The Opening of the American Mind

Also by Lawrence W. Levine

The Unpredictable Past:
   Explorations in American Cultural History

Highbrow/Lowbrow:
   The Emergence of Cultural Hierarchy in America

Black Culture and Black Consciousness:
   Afro-American Folk Thought from Slavery to Freedom

Defender of the Faith: William Jennings Bryan:
   The Last Decade, 1915–1925

The Opening of the American Mind
Canons, Culture, and History

Lawrence W. Levine

Beacon Press
Boston

Beacon Press
25 Beacon Street
Boston, Massachusetts 02108-2892

Beacon Press books
are published under the auspices of
the Unitarian Universalist Association of Congregations.

01 00 99 98 97 96   8 7 6 5 4 3 2 1

Text design by Wesley B. Tanner/Passim Editions
Composition by Electronic Publishing Services, Inc.

Library of Congress Cataloging-in-Publication Data can be found on page 214.

For Richard Hofstadter (1916–1970),
who taught me that there is significance
in all human thought and action

And for the generations of Berkeley students
who have helped me search for it

The dogmas of the quiet past, are inadequate to the stormy present. . . . We must disenthrall ourselves, and then we shall save our country.

Fellow-citizens, *we* cannot escape history.

Abraham Lincoln
Annual Message to Congress, December 1, 1862

Contents

Prologue

In the Spring of 1981 the Vietnam Veterans Memorial Fund announced that the winner of the competition to design a national memorial to Vietnam War veterans was Maya Ying Lin, a twenty-one-year-old Yale undergraduate from Athens, Ohio. Ms. Lin's design, which was chosen over 1,420 other entries, consisted of two 200-foot-long black granite walls arranged in the shape of an elongated V, sloping down in each direction from where they meet until they appear to recede into the earth. The names of the almost sixty thousand American men and women who died in the war were to be inscribed on the walls not in the order of their rank but in the chronological order of their death. The polished black granite was reflective so that visitors, seeing their own images amid the names on the walls, would feel themselves participants rather than mere spectators.

This design, which is now so familiar to us, aroused immediate outrage. In an editorial entitled "STOP THAT MONUMENT" the *National Review* denounced the proposed memorial as "Orwellian glop." The design, it charged, "says that the Vietnam War should be memorialized in black, not in the white marble of Washington. The mode of listing the names makes them individual deaths, not deaths in a cause. They might as well have been traffic accidents." Members of Congress called it a "tombstone" devoid of the proper patriotic spirit. Other critics contrasted the proposed monument with its neighbors, the Washington Monument and the Lincoln Memorial, which, unlike the dark descending walls bearing the names of plain soldiers, were "edifices of white marble rising in massive splendor to honor great American heroes." Testifying before the United States Fine Arts Commission, Tom Carhart complained that the memorial would be an insult to him and his fellow veterans, "a black gash of shame and sorrow, hacked into the national visage." Why, he pleaded, "can't we have something white and traditional and above ground?" The protests led to a compromise: A traditional sculpture and a pole bearing a large American flag would be placed in front of the memorial.[1]

Ultimately, it was neither the flag nor the representational statue of three soldiers that would move the American people; it was the walls bearing name after name of those who never returned from the battlefield. When the memorial opened to the public during the Veterans Day weekend of 1982, tens of thousands of people crowded in front of the walls, reaching out to touch the names cut into the stone, to make paper rubbings of them, to attach letters and flowers to them. "It is already clear that the wall has touched a . . . basic and human strain of response," a reporter observed. "Bearded veterans wearing old fatigue jackets and battle medals can be seen reaching toward the names of remembered dead warriors, running the fingers across the letters. Gray-haired women lean forward and reach and touch." "You have to touch it," one veteran explained. "There's something about touching it."[2]

Within six months the Vietnam Veterans Memorial was the third most heavily visited attraction in Washington, eclipsed only by the Air and Space Museum and the Lincoln Memorial. By 1986 it was—and to this day remains—the most heavily visited memorial in Washington and the model for Vietnam memorials in cities and towns throughout the country. As many as twenty thousand visitors a day touch the names on its walls and leave behind them letters, stuffed animals, medals of honor, photographs, combat boots, and articles of clothing as offerings and messages to those who died. By 1995, forty-eight thousand objects had been gathered by the National Park Service and organized into an ongoing social history collection. "There have always been mementos left at war memorials," Duery Felton, the collection's curator observed, "but not of the intensity and volume that we are receiving. It's unique in that the items were not selected by a museum curator. History is being written from the bottom up, instead of from the top down." And, one should add, this history is being "written" in a most appropriate place: the Washington Mall which, with its many monuments and museums is, as Charles Griswold has noted, "*the* place where the nation conserves its past."[3]

The everyday Americans who for too long had been omitted from the nation's memory and ceremonies had been reinstated despite the cries of critics who were convinced that the national memory should be reserved for white marble pedestals occupied by the great and famous doers of monumental deeds. No one seems to mind the people—the "masses"—when they remain anonymous as they do in the Tomb of the Unknown Soldier at Arlington National Cemetery. But those who planned and designed the Vietnam Veterans Memorial had the audacity to remove the cloak of anonymity from those it was honoring and to name them clearly and permanently. This was the transgression for which they were so heavily criticized and the triumph for which they will be remembered.

The dispute over the Vietnam Memorial was not a random encounter. It was a dramatic instance of a larger struggle over how our past should be conserved, how our memory should function, and where the focus of our attention should be. These confrontations have ranged widely throughout our society from the venues of popular culture to those of formal education, from movie theaters and television studios to libraries and museums. But nowhere has this encounter been more prominent and more divisive than in our colleges and universities. Was there room in our education for the deeds and thoughts, the culture and lore, the history and lives of the disparate array of human beings who made up the American people? Was there space within the halls of our educational institutions for the full range of voices necessary to relate our whole history and the history of those many other lands whose cultures have touched ours profoundly and permanently? Could we rebuild our educational curricula and restructure our educational canons so that they accomplished these complex tasks?

Nor are these encounters unique to our time. Throughout the nineteenth and twentieth centuries American colleges and universities have been engaged in attempts to open themselves to new areas of learning, to new ways of structuring education, and to new constituencies of students among the middle and working classes, women, immigrants, and minorities. These attempts have led to intense struggles within universities over the depth and breadth of their curricula and the nature of their mission.

This is a book about those struggles which I have tried to understand in their historical context. Part I discusses the current critique of and attack upon universities, their faculties, and students. Part II surveys the major debates over the curriculum and the canon during the past two hundred years and provides a framework for seeing the struggles of our own day in a larger setting. Part III examines the bases for many of these debates by exploring the continuities and changes in the ways in which Americans came to comprehend the manner of their national being: How did such a disparate people become *American* and what did that term encompass? It is a book about generations of Americans in institutions of higher education who came to believe along with Abraham Lincoln that "the dogmas of the quiet past, are inadequate to the stormy present," and about the reactions to their attempts to follow Lincoln's advice to "disenthrall" themselves and think and build anew.[4]

It is essential that we understand the current struggles in and around the university in their historical context because only then can we fathom their meaning; only then can we comprehend fully the reason for and the nature of the changes that have been taking place in American universities in the past several decades. Unfortunately, too many Americans currently seem to be engaged in another one of our periodic attempts to escape history by detaching the present from the historical process. We tend to employ two basic strategies to accomplish this escape. The first is what we might call the Flintstonizing of the past after the popular cartoon and recent film *The Flintstones* centering on an imaginary society of cave men and women who resemble us in almost every detail: they drive cars (with stone wheels and foot-pedal power), work in offices replete with bosses and secretaries, speak on telephones (made of sea shells), live in suburban (stone) houses which shelter their nuclear families and their house pets (dinosaurs of the smaller and tamer variety), eat in fast-food restaurants, go on vacations, and on and on. Everything is totally familiar; there is room for progress—better cars and phones and houses—but not for substantial change. This comforting escape from the frequently chaotic dynamic of history validates the present by extending it back into the dim past. In this historical scenario anything that seriously threatens the status quo—from the way we define gender roles, to the subjects we assign our young people to study, to the definitions we give to the idea of culture—endangers not merely contemporary society but all of tradition, all of history.

The second dominant mode of avoiding history—which we might call the Jeremian view of the past after the prophet whose lamentations fill a book of the Scriptures—appears on the surface to be the exact opposite of the Flintstone variety. It accomplishes its illusion through a string of jeremiads which sever contemporary society from the past almost entirely. Thus the present becomes *sui generis:* Never before has there been such disorder, such lack of discipline, such disregard for tradition. Never before have the young shown similar contempt for good sense and for their elders (the repositories of Good Sense). Never before have educators dared to challenge the canons of learning with such abandon and lack of reverence for our cultural heritage. Never before has everything in the realm of culture become so uncompromisingly politicized—so Politically Correct—that teachers and students fear to articulate their views openly and freely. Never before has the educational canon become so diluted by the forced addition of works chosen not for their quality but because of the race or gender of their creators. Never before has the study of the Significant been so dwarfed by the pursuit of the Trivial. Never before have we lived in such a fragmented and inchoate condition in which immigrants and minorities manifest blatant group consciousness and an unwillingness to learn the language, adhere to the traditions, or enter the structures of the larger society.

It is in their implicit denial of the dynamic of historical transformation, it is in their tacit fear of change, it is in their invention of a stable past to which we must pay homage, that both the Flintstonian and Jeremian strategies come together and constitute a complementary escape from history.

But as Lincoln reminded his fellow citizens in 1862, "we cannot escape history."[5] Lincoln had in mind not only the *judgment* of history (the appraisals of future generations), but also the *dynamic* of history. He understood that the Civil War was not an accidental event; it was the product of history. Americans could not avoid the issues at the heart of the war—race, freedom, union, the nature of the economy—for these were part of the thrust of United States history, the results of actions and decisions generations of Americans had taken and made. The only way out of these issues was through them and the only way through them was to confront them with clarity and knowledge. Americans had to understand what was happening to them in the context of what had been happening.

We are as much in need of Lincoln's warning as was his generation; we share similar burdens and opportunities. In recent decades we have come closer than ever before to an understanding of the composition and the nature of that complexity we call the American people. Similarly, we have come much closer to a comprehension of and appreciation for that equally complex phenomenon—American culture—whose existence has been for so long ignored or denigrated or even denied. Alas, we also have come dangerously close at times to listening to those who urge us to close our minds to these new perceptions which are not particularly easy to grasp or live with and which deviate so markedly from many of the certainties and expectations that were once at the core of our education and our understanding. "The greatest enemy of any one of our truths," William James once commented, "may be the rest of our truths."[6] Truths crowd out truths; realities impinge on realities; facts clash with as well as complement each other.

Because the quest to understand the past and the present in their full complexity and ambiguity can be discomfiting and even threatening, there has been opposition to the attempts to seek and articulate multidimensional explanations in such areas as the forging of American identity, the significance of American culture, the nature of the American people, and the role of diverse groups in shaping American consciousness and society. This opposition often takes the form of attacks upon the university which is seen as the primary source of these new explanations.

The university is no longer the site of homogeneity in class, gender, ethnicity, and race. In 1960 only some 6 percent of college students were from minority groups; by 1988 the number had risen to almost 20 percent. In 1960 women earned only 35 percent of the bachelor's degrees and 10 percent of the Ph.D.s conferred; in 1990 they earned 54 percent of the B.A.s and 37 percent of the Ph.D.s. By 1985 27 percent of the faculty in institutions of higher education were women, and more than 10 percent were non-White. And if we remember that during these same years university faculties were expanded by the entry, often for the first time, of East European Jews, Italians, and other ethnic groups from the "wrong" parts of Europe into such humanistic departments as history and literature—the repositories of our memory and our culture—we can achieve a fuller sense of the dynamic of change.[7]

At the University of California at Berkeley, where I have spent most of my teaching career, the ethnic changes in the undergraduate student body have been even more dramatic. With the percentage of White undergraduate students falling from 68.6 percent in 1974 to 32.4 percent twenty years later, Berkeley became the first major state university with a majority of minority students.* Berkeley's experience is an indication of the transformation the entire nation will experience in the near future. While Whites constituted about three-quarters of the United States population in 1995, the Census Bureau estimates that by 2050 they will have declined to barely half of the population with Hispanics comprising almost 25 percent, Blacks about 15 percent, and Asians nearly 10 percent.[8]

The United States has always been a multicultural, multiethnic, multiracial society, but in our own time these truths—and their implications for higher education—have become increasingly difficult to ignore. As the university becomes more open to and representative of the diverse peoples, experiences, traditions, and cultures that compose America, its impulse to find explanations for those parts of our history and our culture we have ignored grows proportionately. It has to enable its students to comprehend the nature of the society they're part of, the history of groups and traditions they will interact with, the meaning of ideas and experiences they will inevitably encounter.

---

*During this twenty-year period Asians increased from 15.8 percent to 39.4 percent, Hispanics from 3.2 percent to 13.8 percent, African Americans from 4.4 percent to 5.5 percent and Native Americans from 0.5 percent to 1.1 percent.

It is precisely because the changes taking place in the nation are so manifest in higher education that universities, along with their faculties and students, have become prime targets for those frustrated by the shape and texture of modern America. The contemporary university with its eclectic faculties and student bodies, its rich array of courses and programs, its dedication to expanding students' understanding of the diverse cultures and societies that surround them, has been drawn into the cultural conflicts that characterize our time. This, as I said above, is not the first time universities have become major players in the nation's culture wars. Although almost every generation has had to fight this battle for greater openness and diversity anew, it is not a new battle and it is essential that we understand its history, context, and significance.

This, then, is a brief book about the *opening* of the American mind from the early nineteenth century until now. It is also a plea on behalf of the steadfastness needed to *keep* our minds open, the courage required to live with the complexities of a deeper understanding of our culture and ourselves, and the honesty vital to an encounter with, rather than an escape from, history.

Acknowledgments

Those who resemble Walt Whitman's "noiseless, patient spider" issuing out of *itself* filament after filament and building its web, may not need to grace their books with lists of acknowledgments. Fortunately, the filaments that constructed this book have not all been issued out of myself; I have been dependent on communities of friends, students, and colleagues, and a number of institutions I am happy to acknowledge, however inadequately, here.

This book began as a presidential address to the Organization of American Historians (OAH) which was delivered at the April 1993 annual meeting in Anaheim, California, and published with a few slight revisions in the *Journal of American History* the following December. The amount of work and engagement that went into that address, and my sense that the materials and issues I dealt with there needed wider circulation, persuaded me to enlarge those original efforts into this book-length essay. I am profoundly indebted to my colleagues in the OAH for presenting me with the occasion to deliver the address in the first place, for the generous and supportive manner in which they received it, and for the numerous suggestions they made for improving it.

In addition to those present in Anaheim, I have been privileged to try out some of these ideas before a wide variety of academic audiences from Colby College in Maine on one side of the country to the Stanford Humanities Center on the other. Members of the Washington, D.C., Seminar on American History and Culture and the Berkeley American Studies Reading Group commented helpfully on portions of this book. In the fall of 1994 I shared some of these thoughts in a lecture delivered at the inaugural ceremonies of the Cultural Studies graduate program at George Mason University whose faculty I had just joined. A year later a much abridged version of this book constituted the substance of the three Carl Becker Lectures I delivered at Cornell University. On each of these occasions my audiences responded with patience and encouragement, and offered suggestions that frequently led me back to the drawing board.

We hear a good deal about the "global village" our world has become, but even though W. B. Carnochan and I were working on many of the same concerns just fifty miles apart, he in Stanford and I in Berkeley, I learned of his work, *The Battleground of the Curriculum: Liberal Education and American Experience,* only after it was published in the summer of 1993. Since the bulk of what has been written on the current struggle over the curriculum and the canon has been from a very different perspective, I derive much encouragement from Professor Carnochan's work and from the work of such other scholars as Michael Bérubé, Henry Louis Gates, Jr., Gerald Graff, Paul Lauter, Francis Oakley, Peter N. Stearns, and John K. Wilson. It would be nice to think that even as I write this others are working on these problems from a number of new vantage points that also differ from the tired and unproductive tendency to paste "politically correct" labels on universities and scholars and to engage in what Carnochan has called the "crisis-mongering [that] has become a national pastime."

This book was largely completed during the academic year 1994–1995 when I was fortunate enough to enjoy a John Simon

Guggenheim Memorial Fellowship and a month's residency at the Rockefeller Foundation's Study and Conference Center in Bellagio, Italy, both of which honors expedited my work significantly. My work also was facilitated by the availability of research funds through the Margaret Byrne Chair at the University of California, Berkeley.

Once again I have been privileged to work with research assistants who aided me with consummate skill and unfailing thoughtfulness. Madelon Powers helped me to orient myself when I was just beginning to think about these issues, and Sara Webber gathered materials and dispensed excellent advice on a number of subjects. Brigitte Koenig worked closely with me on every part of this book. She located sources, aided me in resolving any number of dilemmas, and, with her remarkable critical skills, she commented on and improved the style and the content of each chapter. Her discernment, enthusiasm, and humor helped me maintain my perspective and my good spirits. She was, in short, indispensable and I am deeply grateful to her.

Edward Brown, Jon Gjerde, Elliott Gorn, and Kathleen Moran read all or part of the manuscript and while I was not always wise enough to heed their suggestions, this is a better book because of them. It is a better book as well because of my close friends in diverse departments and programs at the University of California, Berkeley, and George Mason University who stimulate and sustain me on a regular basis.

In the fall of 1993 I had the good fortune to teach a course on "Cultural Identity in American History: Theory and Experience" with my old friend VèVè Clark of Berkeley's African American Studies Department. I have been discussing questions of ethnicity and identity with her since we first met in the 1970s, but our elaborate preparations for and collaboration during the course, as well as our interactions with the wonderfully diverse undergraduates we taught and the talented graduate students who assisted us, were especially helpful in enabling me to explore and rethink many of the issues discussed in Part III of this book, "The Search for the American Identity." Similarly, my understanding of American culture has been sharpened considerably as a result of courses I've had the immense pleasure of teaching with Richard Hutson of Berkeley's English Department.

Sandra Dijkstra was a model of what a literary agent should be. She not only taught me a lot about publishing that I should have known at my advanced age, but didn't, she also had thoughtful things to say about the art of writing history. Andrew Hrycyna of Beacon Press left his mark on this work as he helped me turn my draft into a book with gentle persuasion and acute understanding.

As she has done from my first book in 1965 to this one some thirty years later, my wife Cornelia Levine has been my best critic and my best friend. She was never too tired or too busy to engage in extended conversations with me about all aspects of this work, to read every page of every draft, and, whenever I faltered, to remind me why I was writing it and why I needed to complete it.

A Historian in Wonderland

> *"I could tell you my adventures—beginning from this morning,"* said Alice a little timidly; *"but it's no use going back to yesterday, because I was a different person then."*
>
> *"Explain all that,"* said the Mock Turtle.
>
> *"No, no! The adventures first,"* said the Gryphon in an impatient tone: *"explanations take such a dreadful time."*
>
> Lewis Carroll, *Alice's Adventures in Wonderland*

Through the Looking Glass

The titles of the best-known books on contemporary higher education published in the past decade are instructive:

> *The Closing of the American Mind: How Higher Education Has Failed Democracy and Impoverished the Souls of Today's Students*
> *Profscam: Professors and the Demise of Higher Education*
> *The War Against the Intellect: Episodes in the Decline of Discourse*
> *Tenured Radicals: How Politics Has Corrupted Our Higher Education*
> *Killing the Spirit: Higher Education in America*
> *The Hollow Men: Politics and Corruption in Higher Education*
> *Illiberal Education: The Politics of Race and Sex on Campus*
> *The De-Valuing of America: The Fight for Our Culture and Our Children*
> *Impostors in the Temple: American Intellectuals Are Destroying Our Universities and Cheating Our Students of Their Future*
> *Dictatorship of Virtue: Multiculturalism and the Battle for America's Future*[1]

It's a small growth industry, this jeremiad against the universities and the professoriate, this series of claims that something has

suddenly turned sour in the academe, that the Pure Aims and
Honest Values and True Worth of the past have been sullied and
fouled by politics, by radicals disguised as professors, by academics
consulting only their own interests and completely ignoring those
of the students and the society. The charges go on and on, and the
tone, as these book titles suggest, is relentlessly apocalyptic.

Patrick Buchanan's assertion during the presidential campaign
of 1992 that we were engaged in a war "for the soul of America.
. . . a cultural war, as critical to the kind of nation we will one day
be as was the Cold War itself," is echoed again and again in the
struggle over the university, and these reverberating echoes have
created a culture of hyperbole. The choice facing us today, Roger
Kimball cautioned in his assault on contemporary higher education, is "between culture and barbarism." Thomas Aquinas
College of Santa Paula, California, advertised its "civilized education for the serious student" under a logo featuring a salivating
wolf, teeth bared, wearing an academic mortarboard cap. "Many
in today's academy," the ad warned, "bare their teeth, not only at
our traditions of government, economics, and social order, but
also at the very civilization that gave birth to the university." In
1991 the columnist George F. Will charged that disagreements
over the curriculum were "related battles in a single war, a war of
aggression against the Western political tradition and the ideas
that animate it." He declared that Lynn Cheney, who as head
of the National Endowment for the Humanities was one of the
nation's most vocal critics of universities, was our "secretary of
domestic defense." The foreign adversaries that her husband,
Secretary of Defense Richard Cheney, faced "are less dangerous,
in the long run, than the domestic forces with which she must
deal." What is at stake in the battles among intellectuals on the
American campus, the sociologist Brigitte Berger assured a *Partisan Review* symposium, is nothing less than "the legitimacy of
the Western academic tradition and the cultural values upon
which it rests."[2]

In his journal the *New Criterion,* Hilton Kramer inveighed against allowing "the trash of popular culture" onto the campus and declared, "It is our civilization that we believe to be at stake in this struggle." While Kramer spied disaster in professors wallowing in the muck of popular culture, former Secretary of Education William Bennett accused them of the opposite crime, hating the "vulgar" culture of everyday Americans: "If the middle class likes it—be it conventional morality, patriotism, Ronald Reagan, or even *Rocky,* light beer, cookouts, or Disney World—that alone is enough for many of the elites to disdain it." According to Bennett, this all-out academic assault against the tastes and values of the American people has taken its toll: "We ceased being clear about the standards which we hold and the principles by which we judge. . . . As a result, we suffered a cultural breakdown."[3]

The same double bind applies to the subject of politics. If contemporary academics pay attention to politics they are being political, and if they ignore politics they are being political. In either case they are censured as political advocates rather than scholars. George F. Will has used the term "Academic Marxists" to describe those who envision culture as reflecting such broad societal forces as politics and thus deny what Will calls "the autonomy of culture." To suggest that Shakespeare's *Tempest* comments on the imperialism of Elizabethan England robs the play of its aesthetic qualities and reduces it to "a mere index of who had power and whom the powerful victimized." This works to "strip literature of its authority" and opens the way to "social disintegration, which is the political goal of the victim revolution that is sweeping campuses." On the other hand, the historian Gertrude Himmelfarb has used the same term—"Marxists"—to label social historians who pay *insufficient* attention to politics and ignore Aristotle's admonition that "man is by nature a political animal." Where the old history "features kings, presidents, politicians, leaders, political theorists," she complained, "the new takes as its subject the 'anonymous masses.'" "Marxism," she concluded, "has succeeded . . . in demeaning and denigrating political events, institutions, activities, and ideas."[4]

Whatever the specifics of the charges, contemporary critics of the university agree that higher education in the United States faces a threat more dire than any in its history and they illustrate their charges in a rollicking blizzard of assertions and accusations. In *The Closing of the American Mind*, which spent thirty-one weeks on the *New York Times* best-seller list, sold some 800,000 copies in its original edition, and was the second best-selling hardback book of 1987, Allan Bloom argued that the student, feminist, and Black power movements of the 1960s and 1970s had resulted in the "democratization of the university" which led to "the collapse of the entire American educational structure." His direct historical analogy was with the populism of Nazi Germany. He compared the New Left to Nazi Youth, the Woodstock concert to the Nuremberg Rally, and the professors who "collaborated" with the American student movements to such supporters of Hitler as Martin Heidegger, the Nazi Rector of Freiburg University. In the fall of 1988 at the first national meeting of the conservative National Association of Scholars (NAS), the historian Alan Kors received a standing ovation when he warned that "the barbarians are in our midst" and enjoined his colleagues "to fight them a good long time." At the second national meeting of the NAS in the spring of 1990, Kors received another standing ovation by urging his colleagues to create within their own ranks "the monasteries of a new dark ages, preserving what is worth preserving amid the barbaric ravages in the countrysides and towns of academe."[5]

The journalist Richard Bernstein compared academic multiculturalists to the "Red Guards of China's Great Proletarian Cultural Revolution" and salted his book about the university with words like "terror," "atrocity," "assault," "dictatorship," and "demagogues," while Robert Hughes peppered his with "PC-mongers," "lefty thought police," and "PC claptrap." The late Page Smith called the university "a classic Frankenstein monster" and compared the process of achieving university tenure "to ancient rites of human sacrifice." Not to be outdone, Charles Sykes equated curricular change with "the burning of books," and called the contemporary university a "ghetto of appalling intellectual squalor and mediocrity," inhabited by "the obscurantists, sorcerers, and witch doctors of profthink." In his best-selling *Illiberal Education*, Dinesh D'Souza asserted that by the time students graduate, universities have taught them that "all rules are unjust," that individual rights "should be subordinated to the claims of group interest," that "convenient myths and benign lies can substitute for truth," that "justice is simply the will of the stronger party," that "the university stands for nothing in particular," and that "the multiracial society cannot be based on fair rules that apply to every person."[6]

The very manner of their presentation confirmed the apocalyptic tone of many of these condemnations. *New York Magazine* illustrated John Taylor's attack on "political correctness" in the United States with pictures of Nazi youth smiling into the camera as they burned books in the 1930s and Red Guards in Communist China parading academic "dunces" in the 1960s. In 1995 the front cover of the *San Francisco Examiner Magazine* announced an article on multiculturalism by its senior editor Gary Kamiya featuring a white plaster bust of the German composer Richard Wagner with a red book bearing the title *The Multicultural Handbook* in German gothic print opened like a dunce cap on his head, and on his breast in dripping red letters (ink? blood?) the words: "NO DEAD WHITE EUROMALES."[7]

There is no deeper orthodoxy in the minds of contemporary critics of the university than the notion that the university has been politicized and is now controlled by what Roger Kimball has called "tenured radicals." The scenario is simple and is reiterated so often that it appears to be one of those evident truths not even open for discussion. The New Left of the 1960s, having lost the battle in the streets, retreated to the university which it now dominates. According to Robert Brustein, a Harvard professor of Drama and English, "Many, if not most, of today's PC lead-

ers were active members of the New Left twenty-five years ago."
The very same radical students who "once occupied university
buildings over the Vietnam War, are now officially occupying university offices as professors, administrators, deans, and even presidents." New Left veterans, the historian John Diggins agrees, "are
tenured professors within the system and now have the means of
expounding their ideas to a captive college audience. The New
Left is an idea whose time has passed and whose power has come."
George Roche, the president of Hillsdale College in Michigan,
argues that once they became the "Establishment on campus,"
the political and intellectual radicals of the 1960s "took their lib-
eral-left agenda on race, class, and gender and camouflaged it
under a mantle of 'diversity,' like the nets of fake foliage used to
disguise tanks in Operation Desert Storm." Thus concealed, the
"diversity troops" waged a successful war against traditional values
and academic discipline. "They have fomented . . . a revolution
that is certainly one of the most critical events in modern times."
Wilcomb E. Washburn of the Smithsonian Institution spread the
alarming news that "academic radicals" have been so dominant on
campus that a "small minority" has been able to train "the vast
majority of those who write, broadcast, or engage in supporting
activities in the press, radio, television, cinema and other opinion-
shaping non-academic institutions." One certainly cannot argue
with Roger Kimball when he writes, "It has often been observed
that yesterday's student radical is today's professor or academic
dean." It has indeed![8]

The assumption that large parts of the academe are now controlled by radicals has led to the conviction that the objective
search for truth, which once characterized the university, has been
eclipsed by conscious partisan advocacy. Professors, of course,
have always advocated things in the classroom: sound scholarship, the scientific method, an intelligible writing style, hard work,
reading and more reading, and often even independent thinking.
But we rarely call these things "advocacy." For the most part in
the past one *taught* subjects and approaches and techniques and

scholarly ideals, one did not *advocate* them. There have been periodic exceptions. At the turn of the last century, those teaching Darwinian biology were accused by some of advocacy. During World War I, the teaching of the German language, German literature, or German music was sometimes met by cries of advocacy. Following both world wars, teaching about the Soviet Union or employing a Marxist approach, or even stressing economic causation too vigorously could earn one the same accusation. But it has been left to our own time to normalize what had hitherto been an occasional practice so that entire subjects and whole schools of interpretation are now branded with the hot irons of radical advocacy and political correctness.

Following the lead of Allan Bloom who likened feminism to the "Terror" that followed the French Revolution and who asserted that the "latest enemy of the vitality of classic texts is feminism" since "the Muses never sang to the poets about liberated women," many of these charges have been leveled at women's studies. Page Smith announced in 1990 that by his "rough calculations" there were "approximately" eighty courses focusing on women at the University of California, Santa Cruz, "virtually" all taught by women faculty members. This situation, according to Smith, had some positive consequences: "My impression is that women teachers take a far more personal interest in their students/recruits than do their male counterparts. The older ones play a warm, supportive, mothering role for immature and uncertain young women." But once we move away from mothering and nurturing, the fact that "women have, in effect, seized control over a substantial part of the curriculum," has had uniformly negative results. Smith declared that there are now two Universities of California in Santa Cruz: the "Male Division" where "the traditional pieties still prevail . . . science, objectivity, scholarship," and the "Female Division" where "all pretense of objectivity . . . has been cast aside." Smith's sole documentation for the existence of what he calls "this internal armed feminist camp" is the proliferation of courses in women's studies. Similarly, Charles Sykes counted 50 separate centers devoted to women's issues and 530 programs offering over 30,000 courses in women's studies, and concluded on the basis of this quantitative evidence alone that "obviously women need a vanguard revolutionary elite, just as the proletariat did to lead them to revolutionary consciousness. In its Leninist formulation, this idea is discredited in every capital of Eastern Europe, Moscow not excepted. Miraculously, it is reborn in feminist academia and thus in the curriculum of many of America's elite universities."[9]

When Richard Bernstein of the *New York Times* visited the annual meeting of the American Historical Association in 1987, his sense of the appropriate and significant was offended: "Gone were what I thought of as the Grand Themes, the declines and falls of empires, the waxing and waning of civilizations, the struggles of competing armies, the achievements of Great Men and Women." Instead of the subjects he deemed appropriate, he noted panels on "Women's Definitions of Love Throughout Western History," "Sex, Gender and the Constitution," "Black Women in the Work Force," and "Sodomy and Pederasty Among 19th-Century Seafarers," and without discussing the contents of those papers or the significance of their findings, he concluded that group politics had "replaced even the ideal of disinterestedness," and that "for many historians, history had become advocacy." Once again, the mere presence of certain subjects was all the proof necessary. James Atlas of the *New York Times Magazine* inspected the reading list for one of Stanford's new Culture, Ideas, Values freshman courses in 1989 and reported that along with the Bible, Aeschylus, and Shakespeare, "one finds *With a Pistol in His Hand* by Americo Paredes, *He Who Does Evil Should Expect No Good* by Juana Manuela Gorritti, and something called *Documents from the Tupac Amani Rebellion.*" Atlas fails to tell us what the subject or purpose of the course was and how the readings did or did not fit together to accomplish that purpose. Nor does he demonstrate any familiarity with the latter three books—Paredes's *With a Pistol in His Hand,* for instance, is a superb, original, and deeply

scholarly study of Mexican and Mexican American folk culture
and thought as manifested in a *corrida* (ballad) about a Mexican
bandit. Nevertheless, Atlas concluded that "the presence of such
a reading list . . . makes it hard to dismiss as paranoia Hilton
Kramer's contention that universities are now firmly in the hands
of the radical left." Finding evidence of radicalism in the very title
of books whose substance is not examined has become standard
practice. Again and again, critics trot out the paper "Jane Austen
and the Masturbating Girl," presented by Eve Sedgwick at the
1989 annual meeting of the Modern Language Association. This is
probably one of the most heavily cited and least read scholarly
papers in history. What it actually *says* is never discussed and seems
to be beside the point; its title—its subject—alone suffices as
incontrovertible proof of the advocacy that seriously threatens
the academe.[10]

On the day before Christmas, 1990, Charles Krauthammer in
his nationally syndicated column announced the death of communism and socialism and asked, "What's left of the left?" His
answer: The environmental movement, the antiwar movement,
and the literary theory known as deconstruction. Of the three,
he concluded, deconstruction posed the most serious threat:
"America will survive both Saddam and the snail darter. But the
. . . fracturing . . . of the American idea, poses a threat that no outside agent in this post-Soviet world can match." Roger Kimball
has epitomized this entire mode of thought by charging that such
new subjects and approaches as "women's studies, black studies,
gay studies, . . . deconstruction, poststructuralism, new histori-
cism" are "politically motivated" and contain "a blueprint for a
radical social transformation that would revolutionize every aspect
of social and political life, from the independent place we grant
high culture within society to the way we relate to one another as
men and women."[11]

Fears of an eroding hierarchy and the encroachment of a democratic society into the academe, as reflected in both the curriculum
and the student body, are at the heart of many of the critiques of

contemporary higher education. After reading Plato's *Symposium,* a student came to Allan Bloom "with deep melancholy and said it was impossible to imagine that magic Athenian atmosphere reproduced." Bloom assured him that such experiences "are always accessible. . . . right under our noses, improbable but always present." But only for a small elite. "The real community of man . . . the community of those who seek the truth, of the potential knowers, . . . includes only a few, the true friends, as Plato was to Aristotle." Bloom contrasted this true community with the spirit of democracy, now all too prevalent on our campuses, which tends "to suppress the claims of any kind of superiority." Comparing today's universities with his memories of the halcyon days he spent as a student at Dartmouth College, Martin Anderson has written with disdain of the transformation he claims has taken place over the past few decades: "From the rather small, quiet dignified institutions of rarefied scholarly pursuits and the teaching of a select few," the "hallowed halls of ivy" have "ballooned . . . staffed by hundreds of thousands of men and women who call themselves professors, offering courses to millions of students."[12]

This expanded student body and faculty have brought the outside world within the walls of the university and have radically altered the curriculum according to the critics. "Superman is as worthy of study as Shakespeare," Gertrude Himmelfarb has charged. "Comic books are as properly a part of the curriculum as *Hamlet* or *Macbeth.*" The concern goes beyond popular culture to the inclusion in the curriculum of groups previously ignored. Thus James Atlas complained that the college boards in history "now offer questions on child-rearing practices and the place of women in society," and submitted the following as a disturbing example: "How and why did the lives and status of northern middle-class women change between 1776 and 1876?" Atlas admitted, "It's not a bad question, actually; but how many seventeen-year-olds are prepared to answer it?" The real issue, of course, is the nature of the questions we prepare our students to answer:

Should their education include the lives and culture of everyday people? A traditional liberal arts education, Roger Kimball has asserted, "is unquestionably elitist in the sense that it focuses on the pinnacle of human cultural and intellectual achievement," but no longer is "everyone . . . either interested in or capable of taking advantage of a liberal arts education conceived in this way." On a visit to his beloved Harvard, James Atlas was so bewildered by the existence of English Department courses dealing with politics and literature, women in Victorian society, Blacks and Whites in American culture, the rise of mass culture, and family relations and sexuality in the eighteenth-century novel, that he could only turn to a line of W. B. Yeats: "The world is changed, changed utterly."[13]

The extremity of the charges against the university is easily converted to nostalgia for a better past and a sense of dread concerning the future unless something is done to reverse the course universities are now pursuing. Allan Bloom affords a good example. He longed for the time when the university was concerned with the student's *entire* being and conceived as its function the transference of youthful sexual energies to urges of a more metaphysical nature. A significant number of students used to arrive at the university "physically and spiritually virginal, expecting to lose their innocence there. Their . . . literal lust for knowledge, was what a teacher could see in the eyes of those who flattered him by giving such evidence of their need for him. His own satisfaction was promised by having something with which to feed their hunger, an overflow to bestow on their emptiness. His joy was in hearing the ecstatic 'Oh, yes!' as he dished up Shakespeare and Hegel to minister to their need. Pimp and midwife really described him well." Today's students "sated with easy, clinical and sterile satisfactions of body and soul, . . . hardly walk on the enchanted ground they once did. . . . they do not seek wholeness in the university."[14]

According to Bloom, once there were many students "who actually knew something about and loved England, France,

Germany, or Italy, for they dreamed of living there or thought their lives would be made more interesting by assimilating their languages and literatures." These students have "almost disappeared," to be replaced by those "who are interested in the political problems of Third World countries and in helping them to modernize, with due respect to their old cultures, of course." It is, Bloom grumbled, "the Peace Corps mentality, which is not a spur to learning but to a secularized version of doing good works." Sexual liberation, Bloom maintained, made it impossible for students to learn about their sexual beings from old literature "which from the Garden of Eden on made coupling a very dark and complicated business. On reflection, today's students wonder what all the fuss was about." No longer do they imagine that the sexual plots of such writers as Flaubert, Tolstoy, Shakespeare, or the authors of romantic fiction "could teach them anything about the relations they want to have or will be permitted to have. So they are indifferent." Thirty years ago, Bloom insisted, "university students usually had some early emotive association with Beethoven, Chopin and Brahms, which was a permanent part of their makeup and to which they were likely to respond throughout their lives. This was probably the only regularly recognizable class distinction between educated and uneducated in America." Today, students' musical sensibilities are scarred by rock music which, like all popular culture, Bloom characterized as "pseudo-art" containing "nothing noble, sublime, profound, delicate, tasteful or even decent" with "room only for the intense, changing, crude and immediate." As long as young people "have the Walkman on," Bloom warned, "they cannot hear what the great tradition has to say. And, after its prolonged use, when they take it off, they find they are deaf." In area after area, Bloom portrayed contemporary college students as a generation in serious decline who "know so much less, are so much more cut off from the tradition, are so much slacker intellectually, that they make their predecessors look like prodigies of culture. The soil is ever thinner, and I doubt whether it can now sustain the taller growths."[15]

Much of this nostalgia is fueled by a faulty sense of the history of the American university. We are told again and again that until the 1960s university education was ruled by the study of Western Civilization and a canon of the Great Books. In fact, Great Books and Western Civilization courses enjoyed only a brief ascendancy: they emerged largely after World War I and declined in the decades after World War II. The canon and the curriculum that were supposedly governed by Matthew Arnold's dictum of "the best that has been thought and known in the world . . . the study and pursuit of perfection," were in truth never static and were constantly in the process of revision with irate defenders insisting, as they still do, that change would bring with it instant decline. The inclusion of "modern" writers from Shakespeare to Walt Whitman and Herman Melville came only after prolonged battles as intense and divisive as those that rage today. Thus when John Searle maintains that "until recently" there was no controversy over the existence of a widely agreed upon corpus of writers, knowledge of whom was "essential to the liberal education of young men and women in the United States," he is oversimplifying to the point of distortion, as Part II of this book will demonstrate. What is happening in the contemporary university is by no means out of the ordinary; certainly it is not a radical departure from the patterns that have marked the history of the university—constant and often controversial expansion and alteration of curricula and canons and incessant struggle over the nature of that expansion and alteration.[16]

None of these realities stop James Atlas from asserting: "The Great Books. The best that is known and thought in the world. The canon," were "until a few years ago . . . our educational mandate." We would all benefit if those who tell us where to go understood more clearly where we have been. Atlas, who attended Harvard from 1967 to 1971 and is grateful for what he gained from his years there, can't help longing for an earlier, more glorious day: "What my classmates and I managed to learn in those four years couldn't begin to compare with the knowledge absorbed by earlier generations of students, for whom the study of literature included the study of Greek and Latin classics in the original." Fortunately, we can turn directly to the students he envies who, while they did indeed read the "classics" in the original Greek and Latin, read them not as works of literature but as examples of *grammar,* the rules of which they studied endlessly and by rote. James Freeman Clark, who received his Harvard A.B. in 1829, complained, "No attempt was made to interest us in our studies. We were expected to wade through Homer as though the Iliad were a bog. . . . Nothing was said of the glory and grandeur, the tenderness and charm of this immortal epic. The melody of the hexameters was never suggested to us." Henry Adams proclaimed his years at Harvard from 1854 to 1858 "wasted" and exclaimed in his autobiography: "It taught little, and that little ill. . . . Beyond two or three Greek plays, the student got nothing from the ancient languages." Adams wrote of himself: "He could not afterwards remember to have heard the name of Karl Marx mentioned, or the title of 'Capital.' He was equally ignorant of Auguste Comte. These were the two writers of his time who most influenced its thought." "The entire work of the four years," Adams concluded, "could have been easily put into the work of any four months in after life."[17]

Atlas is on equally shaky ground when he locates the Golden Age at my alma mater. The City College of New York "of forty or fifty years ago," he tells us, operated on such a high plane of excellence that it "seems infinitely remote in time" and we, with our debased standards, cannot even imagine its lofty existence. "Things have gone too far," he laments. " . . . We're on the verge of a new barbarism." Atlas's bleak conclusion is based upon the degradation of higher education he and his fellow critics are convinced has taken place in our own time. Here, for example, is a description in *Newsday* of the university in which I have spent most of my teaching career: "Our first major university with a multiracial, white-minority student body, Berkeley has become a tense no-man's-land of mutually exclusive cultural turfs, where

Western civilization is being reduced to something called European-American ethnic studies, and where white students anxiously watch their every word to avoid 'politically incorrect' speech."[18]

In the face of statements like these, which by now are quite common, I feel like Alice in Wonderland living in a topsy-turvy universe that has little to do with my experiences and understanding. Convinced by everything I know and have seen that the American academic world is doing a more thorough and cosmopolitan job of educating a greater diversity of students in a broader and sounder array of courses covering the past and present of the worlds they inhabit than ever before in its history, I walk through the Looking Glass and find myself surrounded by those who see our enterprise as unhealthy and unreliable, built not on the solid foundations of serious inquiry and innovative approaches but on the sands of fashion and politics and coercion.

Both the City College of New York (CCNY) and the University of California at Berkeley have been institutions of the greatest importance in my life. I was a history major at CCNY from 1950 to 1955, the very years Atlas points to as a Pinnacle we can hardly see through the fog of our own decline. I subsequently taught at Berkeley for thirty-two years, from 1962 to 1994, the very years of the presumed Great Decline of the American university. The profound debt I owe City College, which changed my life for the better in a myriad of ways and enabled me not only to dream dreams but to fulfill them, cannot alter the fact that the education I received there does not begin to compare in any respect (save the quality of my classmates) to the one I've been part of during the past few decades at Berkeley. The history courses I took at CCNY required that I read very fat and exceedingly dull and predictable textbooks which rarely diverged from a straightforward narrative, political, Mover-and-Shaker, Whiggish historical approach which recounted a story of never-ending progress. I learned almost nothing about workers, slaves, immigrants, children, or women. I learned almost nothing about how people acted in their families, their churches, their homes, their places of work, what they did with their leisure time, how they felt about their lives and the lives of those about them. I learned nothing about Africa or Asia after the ancient period, nothing about South America and the Caribbean after the Age of Discovery, nothing about the indigenous cultures that once inhabited the very territory I was now living in, nothing about Canada or Australia, nothing about Eastern or Southern Europe after the Classical Era. Vast geographical areas encompassing most of the world's surface, entire cultures, whole peoples remained a wasteland to me and most of my peers.

I clutched my bachelor's degree as I left City College to enter a world most of whose peoples and cultures I knew virtually nothing about. Students at Berkeley are both more burdened and more privileged. They have an array of courses to choose from and requirements to meet that had no parallels in my undergraduate career. They have to read far more than we did, and generally write more as well, and they are treated to a spectrum of history encompassing more peoples and subjects and realities than we could have even imagined in my generation. The depth and range and diversity and sophistication of history education today simply exceeds anything I experienced in my student days. I certainly have not seen as much progress as I had hoped in most aspects of American life, and I have seen almost none in far too many, but higher education has been a happy exception.

It is precisely these developments that trouble so many of the critics whose lament is less about politics in the classroom than about the cultural changes that have taken place in the university. The advocacy they complain about most vigorously is cultural rather than political in nature. It is the *openness* of the contemporary university that is so threatening and the complexity of the education available to students today that is so disturbing to the university's most vigorous detractors. The title of Bloom's *The Closing of the American Mind* was paradoxical. His real target was what he called "the recent education of openness." He characterized the contemporary university as "open to all kinds of

men, all kinds of lifestyles, all ideologies," and thus "closed" to the
absolute truths of the classical writings and great books that alone
constitute true education. Bloom identified the real villain as cultural relativism which he defined as the conviction that all societies
and values and beliefs are as "good" as all others. Bloom's anxiety
was not relieved by the fact that what cultural relativism commonly taught students is not to make a simple-minded equation
between everything as equal, but rather to be open to the reality
that all peoples and societies have cultures which we have to
respect to the extent that we take the trouble to understand how
they operate and what they believe. Bloom found this perspective
no less dangerous since it opens students to the possibility that
their culture is not necessarily superior and potentially weakens the
conviction that Western culture and "Civilization" are synonymous. He condemned contemporary education for "destroying
the West's universal or intellectually imperialistic claims, leaving it
to be just another culture." Bloom insisted that the permanent
and natural state between cultures is one of Darwinian competition. Values, he argued, "can only be asserted or posited by over
coming others, not by reasoning with them. Cultures have different *perceptions,* which determine what the world is. They cannot
come to terms. There is no communication about the highest
things. . . . Culture means a war against chaos *and* a war against
other cultures."[19]

Writing of the demands to include in the curriculum "populations and points of view that have been 'marginalized,'" "popular
culture," "the tradition essential to *un*educated Americans,"
"native American influences," "Africa," Roger Kimball warned
that "a swamp yawns open before us, ready to devour everything.
The best response to all this—and finally the only serious and
effective response—is not to enter these murky waters in the first
place. As Nietzsche observed, we do not refute a disease. We resist
it." Richard Bernstein characterized the efforts to demystify
Christopher Columbus—whom he calls "our William the Con-
queror, our Joan of Arc, our Alexander Nevsky"—begun over a

hundred years ago during the celebration of the four-hundredth anniversary of Columbus's voyage and revived with much greater force in 1992, as attempts "to replace healthy nation-building myths with dangerous quests for the complicated truth." Commenting on proposed new curricula for New York elementary and secondary schools, James Atlas lamented, "From now on it won't be enough to know the capital of Idaho or who Pocahantas was; seventh-graders will be expected to know why they should know these facts and not others: 'The subject matter content should be *treated as socially constructed* and therefore tentative—as is all knowledge.' Deconstructionism comes to P.S. 87." I can't refrain from commenting that if this be "deconstructionism," I wish it had come to Junior High School 115 when I was a student there in the 1940s. We had no idea why we were learning what we learned, no clue to how and to what end the facts fed to us were chosen. It was this ignorance of *why* that made history such a perennially dreary subject to legions of students and that makes so many adults to this day, when they hear that I'm a historian, mumble with a combination of guilt and aggression, "History was always my least favorite subject," or, "I *hated* history in school."[20]

The "traditional" curriculum that prevailed so widely in the decades between the World Wars, and whose decline is lamented with such fervor by the conservative critics, ignored most of the groups that compose the American population whether they were from Africa, Europe, Asia, Central and South America, or from indigenous North American peoples. The primary and often exclusive focus was upon a narrow stratum of those who came from a few Northern and Western European countries whose cultures and mores supposedly became the archetype for those of all Americans in spite of the fact that in reality American culture was forged out of a much larger and more diverse complex of peoples and societies. In addition, this curriculum did not merely teach Western ideas and culture, it taught the *superiority* of Western ideas and culture; it equated Western ways and thought with "Civilization" itself. This tendency is still being championed by contemporary critics of the university. "Is it Eurocentric to believe the life of liberty is superior to the life of the beehive?" Charles Krauthammer inquired in his justification of the European conquest of the Americas. Without pretending to have studied the cultures of Asia or Africa in any depth, Secretary of Education William Bennett did not hesitate to inform the faculty and students of Stanford University that "the West is a source of *incomparable* intellectual complexity and diversity and depth."[21]

To say that a curriculum that questions these parochial assumptions is somehow anti-Western or anti-intellectual is to misunderstand the aims of education. If in fact the traditions of Western science and humanities mean what they say, modern universities are performing precisely the functions institutions of higher learning should perform: to stretch the boundaries of our understanding; to teach the young to value our intellectual heritage not by rote but through comprehension and examination; to continually and perpetually subject the "wisdom" of our society to thorough and thoughtful scrutiny while making the "wisdom" of other societies and other cultures accessible and subject to comparable scrutiny; to refuse to simplify our culture beyond recognition by limiting our focus to only one segment of American society and instead to open up the *entire* society to thoughtful examination.

To require more careful study and more convincing documentation for the charges against the university is not to be pedantic or picayune; it is to hold the critics of the university to the same scholarly standards and the same humanistic values they claim the university itself has abandoned. The irony is that the critics of the contemporary university too often have become parodies of the very thing they're criticizing: ideologues whose research is shallow and whose findings are widely and deeply flawed by exaggerated claims, vituperative attacks, defective evidence, and inadequate knowledge of the history of the university in the United States and of the process by which canons and curricula have been formed and reformed since the beginning of American higher education.

While performing the high task of protecting knowledge and scholarly standards against "barbarians," it is obviously not always possible to observe the purest scholarly standards oneself. Dinesh D'Souza's "research" technique, for example, is summed up by the following incident. While visiting the Berkeley campus of the University of California, he wanted to speak with "Asian American students" as part of his investigation. Students of Asian ancestry then constituted roughly one-third of the undergraduates at Berkeley, but D'Souza had trouble locating interviewees: "It is not easy to find an Asian student willing to talk at Berkeley. I passed up two or three who would talk only on condition of anonymity. I approached one student waiting for the library to open, but he was too eager not to miss a minute of reading time. Eventually I found Thuy Nguyen, a cheerful woman who turned out to be a student at UC-Davis. She knew all about Berkeley, though; she was visiting her friend Cynthia Dong, an undergraduate there." Thus his *entire* direct testimony from "Berkeley" students of Asian descent—a designation covering a wide variety of peoples and cultures—comes from a student enrolled not at Berkeley but at the University of California at Davis, a campus sixty miles away. Ironically, D'Souza's approach is all too typical of those whose concern about the declining standards and ideals of the academic world has led them to level blistering attacks against it.[22]

After a tour of universities Charles Sykes reported back that "tens of thousands of books and hundreds of thousands of journal articles . . . bloat libraries with masses of unread, unreadable, and worthless pablum." Alas, we never learn whether Mr. Sykes knows this because he himself has performed the heroic task of carefully examining the tens of thousands of books and hundreds of thousands of articles, or if he is synthesizing the Herculean labors of other investigators who remain anonymous, or if he is merely *assuming* that so many books and articles that sit so inertly on library shelves simply *must* be "worthless pablum." Robert Hughes too can't resist the trap of pretending to be able to sum up the scholarly world without having done more than dip the edge of a toenail into it. "With certain outstanding exceptions like Edward Said, Simon Schama or Robert Darnton," he declared, "relatively few of the people who are actually writing first-rate history, biography or cultural criticism in America have professorial tenure." Since in his entire volume Hughes cites only six works of history directly in his notes, it is impossible to discern how he arrived at this ludicrous judgment of the discipline of history which is in one of its most exciting and original periods and has in the past several decades produced large numbers of significant works that have advanced our thinking about the past considerably.[23]

Without taking the trouble to conduct an actual investigation, Martin Anderson, a Fellow at the Hoover Institution, decided: "The work of scholars that is relevant to the critical issues facing Americans is almost nonexistent." This self-generated observation led him to the conclusion that "taken as a whole, academic research and writing is the greatest intellectual fraud of the twentieth century." Based upon precisely the same sort of self-referential "analysis," the historian Page Smith concluded that "the vast majority of the so-called research turned out in the modern university is essentially worthless," though obviously he could have had no actual familiarity with "the vast majority" of university research, most of which is in fields he knew nothing about. Similarly, Allan Bloom presented no evidence whatever to document his assertions that students today appreciate classical music less than they did thirty years ago, or that sexual liberation has robbed them of their ability to relate to the novels of the past, or that students no longer think about or want to visit the countries of Western Europe. Bloom's "research," apart from his own limited personal experience, was primarily internal, conducted largely in the archives of his own mind and the precincts of the sensibilities of the ancient writers as he envisioned them.[24]

In his influential polemic *Tenured Radicals,* Roger Kimball spoke about the "decanonization" of dead, White, European men in recent years but presented no evidence that writers like Shakespeare are actually studied less now than they were before the 1960s. In fact, the most exhaustive surveys of college and university literature courses conducted in 1984–85 and again in 1990 provide no documentation for this accusation made so frequently by conservative critics. The earlier survey concluded that "courses are added to expand the curriculum, not to replace traditional offerings, which remain in place as core requirements for the English major." Of the courses that 80 percent of the English departments insisted their majors take, the three most frequently required were survey courses in British literature, American literature, and Shakespearian drama. The 1990 survey of over nine hundred English teachers indicated that courses in nineteenth-century American literature featured such authors as Nathaniel Hawthorne, Henry David Thoreau, Herman Melville, and Ralph Waldo Emerson, while previously neglected writers like Frederick Douglass and Harriet Beecher Stowe made their way into the curriculum very gradually. "The major works and authors remain preeminent in the courses surveyed," the report concluded. The ways in which curricular change and tradition can and do coexist and constitute the substance of the contemporary university are simply ignored in the impassioned culture of hyperbole which pictures Alice Walker and Toni Morrison displacing Shakespeare.[25]

Like Allan Bloom, Kimball and many of his fellow critics jump from rhetoric to assumption, from assumption to assertion, from assertion to fact. Author after author, critic after critic have recited the catechism concerning how the New Left has captured the academic world. One searches in vain for evidence, for citations, for documentation. Some truths, it seems, are too obvious to require the needless paraphernalia of scholarship. But not too obvious to need constant reiteration so that once again the unproven assertion becomes "documented" through the sheer force of repetition. In 1992, the historian John Diggins asserted that "in the field of American history . . . a liberal Ph.D. who subscribed to consensus instead of class conflict, or a white male conservative who admired

Madison more than Marx, had about as much chance of getting hired on some faculty as Woody Allen of starting as point guard for the Knicks." Though Diggins's claim was unaccompanied by any evidence whatever, Lynn Cheney in her 1992 report as chairman of the National Endowment for the Humanities cited it as a "fact" to document her own allegation that a political agenda now often dominated universities and their faculties. Similarly, Professor Jerry Z. Muller has written that political correctness "is a consequence of the institutionalization within the academy of a cohort of New Leftists who came of age politically in the 1960s, who lecture on egalitarianism while practicing elitism, and who exert disproportionate influence through their organizational zeal and commitment to academic politics," and cited Diggins's own totally unsupported assertion that the New Left dominates as his sole "proof." This kind of uninformed and under-researched generalizing is done ostensibly *in defense* of the university by those who seem to understand, or at least to care, little about its purposes, standards, and approaches.[26]

Charges of political advocacy against the university are made also through the process of transforming norms into extremes. Hostility to the writings of "Dead White European Males" is attributed to any scholar who would supplement the canon with the work of those who have been traditionally excluded from it. Afrocentrism and multiculturalism are made synonymous by simply ignoring the large and sophisticated body of recent scholarship on ethnicity which has nothing to do with Afrocentrism *or* Eurocentrism. Practices and processes that have long exemplified the academe are made to appear to be the contemporary fruits of advocacy. Thus vigorously debating the orthodoxies of prior days, or supplementing and replacing canonical texts and subjects, or altering and experimenting with curricula, or using abstruse theories and complex language, or constructing courses to accommodate the changing nature of the student body, or responding to the major social, cultural, and political forces of the day are treated as evidence of the university's current degradation when in fact they have been endemic in the American academic world. Peter Shaw has complained of "resistance to authority of all kinds" in the modern university: "Literary critics rejected traditional interpretations, scholars found the formal limitations of their disciplines stifling, and humanists objected to the established canon of great works."[27] This condition, of course, is hardly peculiar to our own time but has been an evolving characteristic of American universities throughout the nineteenth and twentieth centuries. Universities are about teaching the methods and dispositions necessary to criticize, question, and test authority.

Similarly, when Gertrude Himmelfarb criticizes many of her fellow historians for daring to "impose upon the past their own determinacy," for acting as if "the past has to be deconstructed and constructed anew," she is, in fact, describing the well-established process of historiography.[28] Historians have always reconstructed the past on the basis of new information, new research, new theories, new approaches, new understandings; on the basis of what the historian Jack Hexter once called the "tracking devices" of their own time. The current emphasis on social and cultural history which so troubles contemporary critics is no more permanent than were past emphases on political, intellectual, economic, or diplomatic history. Neither is it any more—or less—politically motivated. It reflects, as earlier historiographies have reflected, the questions, problems, issues that touch our time and help us make sense of the world. It also reflects the fact that history today is written, as it has always been written, by human beings who are part of their own societies and cultures.

Perhaps the most common of the charges that the contemporary university is guilty of behavior that differentiates it qualitatively from its predecessors and makes it an exception in the history of American higher education are those revolving around what has been called "political correctness" (PC) which has allegedly cast a pall on freedom of expression and action on the American campus. Lynn Cheney has argued that today's students "can disagree with professors. But to do so is to take a risk."[29] In fact, when was it *not* risky for a socialist student to confront her economics professor who was teaching about the wonders of the free market, for an atheist student to confront his professor of religion who was teaching about the wonders of monotheism, or for African American students to confront their professor of history who was teaching about the wonders of the Founding Fathers, many of whom were slaveholders? This has always been the case in the university. Those professors who would welcome vigorous debate and disagreement on fundamentals often fail to get it either because students don't think this is their place, or because of those of their colleagues who don't welcome it and have taught students to repress their dissident urges. Students have always had to learn to accommodate to the whims and prejudices of professors, to the attitudes and sensitivities of fellow students, and to the values and beliefs of the larger society; to, that is, the complex of considerations that today is referred to much too simply as "political correctness."

The trouble with critics like Cheney is that they have made this long-standing condition in the academe a partisan one (unique to the Left) and an exceptional one (unique to our time). From reading Cheney and most of her fellow critics, you would never dream that there existed a conservative Republican professor or a centrist Democratic professor who stifled freedom of thought and inquiry in the classroom, who intimidated students into silence, who felt it was a student's function to listen and a professor's to dominate the discourse, who was confident of having the True Word to impart to a captive student audience. The problem Cheney is describing—of students fearing to risk debate—is neither new nor confined to one part of the political spectrum, nor is it unique to our time, nor is it particularly virulent in our time, nor does it really characterize the contemporary university which is a more varied, more open, more dynamic place to be in and near than ever before. This problem is inherent in the university which is a dual institution: on the one hand a center of free inquiry and discourse, on the other hand a center of intellectual authority—

two characteristics that don't mesh easily and often lead to contra-dictory or inconsistent behavior. Ironically, it is most often Cheney's fellow conservative critics who have invoked authority in their vision of the classroom. Thus Gertrude Himmelfarb has argued that "it is reasonable and proper to ask students, even scholars, . . . to accept, at least provisionally, until disproved by powerful evidence, the judgment of posterity about great writers and great books. This calls for an initial suspension of private judg-ment in favor of authoritative opinion, the collective opinion of generations."[30]

It surely was much simpler when the university community was a homogeneous one, not because there was more freedom but because homogeneity ensured that there was more unanimity about what constituted acceptable ideas and behavior; because, that is, there was *more*, not less, of what today is called political correctness. When Allan Bloom blamed the radical students of the 1960s for opening the university to the "vulgarities present in soci-ety at large," he conveniently ignored the truth that long before the student movements universities had hardly transcended the larger society's "vulgarities" but had in fact mirrored its often prejudiced, repressive, and "politically correct" attitudes toward gender, race, and ethnicity in their admissions policies, their hiring practices, and their curricula.[31]

But the American university no longer is and never again will be homogeneous, and much of what we have seen recently in terms of speech codes and the like are a stumbling attempt to adapt to this new heterogeneity. The major consequence of the new heterogeneity on campuses, however, has not been repres-sion but the very opposite—a flowering of ideas and scholarly innovation unmatched in our history. Charles Sykes quotes the educator Robert Maynard Hutchins's dictum that the liberal arts should free the student "from the prison-house of his class, race, time, place, background, family, and even his nation," and goes on to argue that universities today have reversed Hutchins's defin-ition by focusing on race, class, gender, and sexual orientation.[32]

On the contrary, today's universities with their diverse student bodies, faculties, and curricula have done more to free us from the confines of self-absorption than Hutchins could have imagined. The problem with Hutchins's vision is that like Bloom's, it was coupled to a homogeneous university community of faculty and students largely from the same class and background who were allowed to assume that *they* were the model and everyone else the deviants, that *they* possessed culture which everyone else lacked. What so troubles many conservatives is the modern university's presumption in believing that it can actually educate a wide array of people and help free them from the prison house of stereotypes and assumptions—those they hold of others and those others hold of them.

The British historian Sir Lewis Namier observed that "the crowning attainment of historical study is a historical sense—an intuitive understanding of how things do not happen." It is exactly this understanding of how things do *not* happen that the leading critics of the contemporary university lack. Thus they freely spin their facile theories of how the survivors of the New Left lost the political wars but won their ultimate triumph by capturing the university and transforming it from an institution of culture and learning to a high-handed and inflexible purveyor of Political Correctness. The problem with such notions—aside from the fact that they are promulgated, to borrow Carl Becker's memorable phrase, without fear and without research—is that they are telling examples of how things do not happen. Universities in the United States are not transformed by small cabals of political and social radicals who somehow (the process is never revealed) capture venerable private and public institutions of higher learning, convert them to their own agendas, overwhelm and silence the vast majority of their colleagues while boards of regents and trustees benignly look on, and mislead generations of gullible and passive college youth who are robbed of their true heritage and thus compelled to stumble forth into the larger world as undereducated and uncultured dupes mouthing the platitudes taught them by the band of radical mesmerists posing as college professors. "I have never fully understood the notion that faculty could brainwash me into believing whatever they wanted me to," a Stanford undergraduate testified. "Reading Hitler did not make me a fascist; reading Sartre did not make me an existentialist. Both simply enabled me to think about those philosophies in ways I hadn't previously." It should not take a great deal of reflection to realize that neither college students nor college faculties nor college administrations operate in the manner posited by the apocalyptic and conspiratorial views of the contemporary university. This is not how things happen in the American university and to comprehend why some people are convinced that they do we might ponder Richard Hofstadter's notions of the "paranoid style" in American politics.[33]

In no sense did Hofstadter equate what he called the paranoid style with psychological pathology. He argued that while clinical paranoia describes an individual who is convinced of the existence of a hostile and conspiratorial world "directed specifically *against him*," the paranoid style involves belief in a conspiracy "directed against a nation, a culture, a way of life." Hofstadter found this style recurring throughout American history in the anti-Masonic and anti-Catholic crusades, and in such manifestations of anti-Communism as McCarthyism and the John Birch Society. But there is nothing particularly retrograde about the style; one can find it in aspects of abolitionism, of Populism, and of antiwar movements as well. It is less tied to particular political goals than to a way of seeing the world, a way of understanding how things work by invoking the process of conspiracy. "The paranoid spokesman," according to Hofstadter, "sees the fate of this conspiracy in apocalyptic terms. . . . He is always manning the barricades of civilization. He constantly lives at a turning point: it is now or never in organizing resistance to conspiracy. Time is forever just running out. . . . The apocalypticism of the paranoid style runs dangerously near to hopeless pessimism, but usually stops just short of it."

I would argue that this manner of envisioning reality has frequently characterized those who resisted the changes taking place in American higher education, and never more so than during the past several decades. Perhaps the most unfortunate aspect of this mode of analysis is not merely that it's incorrect but that it's so simple and pat and that we learn little, if anything, from it. "We are all sufferers from history," Hofstadter concluded, "but the paranoid is a double sufferer, since he is afflicted not only by the real world, with the rest of us, but by his fantasies as well."[34]

What is wrong with the dominant critiques is not that they are mistaken in every instance, nor that there aren't things to criticize in contemporary universities. Of course there are. We need to integrate learning more fully and to have more sequential courses that build on one another. We need to minimize the use of inaccessible jargon wherever possible, particularly in those fields where jargon has become a way of life. We need to make a greater effort to communicate with colleagues in other disciplines, with students, and with the general public. We need to ensure that teaching ability is considered seriously in all faculty personnel decisions. We need to learn how to respond to the considerable challenge of teaching the most wide-ranging and heterogeneous body of students in the history of American higher education. The problem is that the charges against the university are so hyperbolic, so angry, so conspiracy-minded, and so one-sided they can find almost nothing positive to say. They see little if any good coming out of the new research and teaching on race and gender, the multifaceted study of American culture, the attempts to more completely understand the world and its peoples and cultures, the exciting development of a student body and faculty that are increasingly becoming more representative of the nation's population.

There *is* fragmentation in the United States; there *is* distrust; there *is* deep anger—and much of this is reflected in and acted out in universities, but none of it is *caused* by universities or by professors or by young people. Nevertheless, all three are easy scapegoats for the problems of the larger society. The many changes taking place in the nation's universities have created awkward moments pregnant with the possibilities of progress but also containing an abundance of room for egregious mistakes, and universities have had their share of both. But to collect dozens of anecdotes illustrating the stumbling of many universities in the face of new pressures and challenges—while ignoring all of their many successful adjustments and innovations—and to parade these stories forth as indicative of the great problem we face is mistaken. Those who do so disregard the fact that the real fragmentation confronting this society has nothing to do with the university, which is one of the more successfully integrated and heterogeneous institutions in the United States, and everything to do with the reality that forms of fragmentation—social, ethnic, racial, religious, regional, economic—have been endemic in the United States from the outset. In our own time this historic fragmentation has been exacerbated because a significant part of our population has been removed from the economy and turned into a permanent underclass with no ladders leading out of its predicament and consequently little hope.

Americans' complicated and ambivalent attitudes toward the university have created the myth that universities are not part of the "real" world, and many professors, pleased at the notion that they were apart from and therefore more "objective" about the surrounding society, have been willing to go along with this illusion and to varying extents have even come to believe it. In truth, as this study will illustrate again and again, universities are never far removed from the larger society. To have a literature of crisis built upon the university and the young as *the* enemy, as *the* creators of fragmentation, discontent, and social turmoil, is so bizarre as to almost, but not quite, defy understanding. Rather than face the complex of reasons for our present state of unease, it is easier and certainly much more comforting to locate the source of our dilemma in an institution—the university—that has always been deeply suspect in the United States, in a group—professors—

who have always been something of an anomaly in a theoretically egalitarian land, and in a generation—college youth—who have always made us nervous because they never *seem* to be our exact replicas.

The trouble with the widespread apocalyptic view of the sudden takeover of the university by forces essentially alien to its basic spirit is that this vision removes the American university from the context of its own extended history and transforms long-term processes of change and development into short-term accidents. When the Mock Turtle asked Alice to explain where she came from, the Gryphon exclaimed impatiently, "No, no! The adventures first, explanations take such a dreadful time."[35] Contemporary critics of the university have shown a similar impatience. Explanations *do* take time, but they remain essential. To understand where the university is we have to understand where it has been and how its present state was constructed. There is no quicker or easier way to proceed; to fathom today requires some awareness of yesterday. In the process we will learn not only about higher education, we will discover truths about our culture and, hopefully, about ourselves as well.

Learning and Legitimacy

There is only one subject-matter for education, and that is Life in all its manifestations.

Alfred North Whitehead, *The Aims of Education*

The Discipline and Furniture of the Mind:
The Clash Over The Classical Curriculum

The best response to critics of the modern American university is the history of the university itself. The best means of comprehending that history is to begin with the classical curriculum.

Throughout the colonial period, American colleges were characterized by a homogeneous model; they were, as one student of education has called them, "copies of copies": the American rendition of the English adaptation of the Renaissance revision of the medieval curriculum. Institutions of higher education in America began their existence suffused with a religious ethos and purpose and firmly in the grip of the classical curriculum, which consisted of Latin, Greek, sometimes Hebrew, mathematics, natural philosophy, moral philosophy, and logic. All students studied the same subjects at the same time with the class in which they entered college. Thus the entire four-year undergraduate curriculum occupied only one page of the 1829–1830 Yale College catalogue.[1]

The curriculum was fixed and finite simply because truth itself was assumed to be fixed and finite. When the first insistent demands for curricular reform were heard in the early decades of the nineteenth century, Yale College appointed a committee to study the feasibility of abolishing the requirement in ancient languages.

The Yale Report of 1828 rejected the suggestion out of hand. The end of a college education, it asserted, was "the *discipline* and the *furniture* of the mind; expanding its powers, and storing it with knowledge," with the emphasis always upon discipline rather than information, and for this purpose there was nothing equal to the classical languages and mathematics. The study of the classics, the report's authors insisted, "forms the most effectual discipline of the mental faculties. . . . Every faculty of the mind is employed; not only the memory, judgment, and reasoning powers, but the taste and fancy are occupied and improved."[2]

The traditional classical curriculum was conceived to be not a matter of choice but an imperative. "Experience has shown," John M. Mason, a trustee of Columbia College, declared in 1805, "that with the study or neglect of the Greek and Latin languages, sound learning flourishes or declines. It is now too late for ignorance, indolence, eccentricity, or infidelity to dispute what has been ratified by the seal of ages. Whoever shall deny the superiority of the ancient classics . . . will forfeit his claim to the reputation of a scholar." "The single consideration that divine truth was communicated to man in the ancient languages, ought to put this question at rest," the Yale Report observed, but if more temporal evidence was necessary, it invited its readers to "let a page of Voltaire be compared with a page of Tacitus." Should Greek and Latin ever be given a "secondary place" in the curriculum, Yale College would "sink into a mere academy," its degrees "would become valueless," and it would become "directly accessary to the depression of the present literary character of our country." The results would be that "the diffusion of intelligence among the people would be checked; the general standard of intellectual and moral worth lowered; and our civil and religious liberty jeoparded." These certainties were by no means confined to the Eastern elite. In 1820 the *Western Review* warned Transylvania University in Kentucky that if Latin and Greek should ever cease to be taught in our universities, and the study of Cicero, Demosthenes, Homer, and Virgil thought unnecessary, "we should regard mankind as fast sinking into absolute barbarism, and the gloom of mental darkness as likely to increase until it should become universal."[3]

The passions that burned in the administrators and faculty of American colleges had more to do with preservation and nurturing than discovery and advancement. During his inauguration as president of Princeton in 1854, John Maclean declared: "We shall not aim at innovations. . . . no chimerical experiments in education have ever had the least countenance here." At nearby Princeton Theological Seminary, Professor Charles Hodge went even further; at the celebration of his half-century of service in 1872, he proudly proclaimed that "a new idea never originated in this Seminary." In Cincinnati Lyman Beecher warned the new western colleges that should they allow "the spirit of innovation" to influence them "the day of our downfal [sic] will soon be at the door, and nothing remain to us but to wade back through seas of blood, from anarchy to despotism."[4]

Subjects outside the golden circle of the classical curriculum—the biological sciences, modern languages, modern literature, modern history (and "modern" of course meant everything since the ancient Greeks and Romans)—were either not available or available without credit and only at the students' own initiative. In 1841 the Yale catalogue announced: "Gentlemen well qualified to teach the modern languages are engaged by the Faculty to give instruction in these branches to those students who desire it, at their own expense." Similarly, the 1862–63 Columbia College catalogue announced a series of lectures by the well-known botanist John Torrey "at such hours as will not interfere with the regular studies of the undergraduates."[5]

Although the Yale Report helped to sustain the classical canon at Yale and many other colleges throughout the country for much of the nineteenth century, it hardly "put this question at rest." Faced with demands for reform, as the century progressed colleges grudgingly offered alternative subjects for credit in one of two ways: through such separate schools as the Sheffield Scientific

School at Yale and the Lawrence Scientific School at Harvard, which never attained the prestige of their parent institutions, or as part of such new and less reputable degree programs as the bachelor of science, the bachelor of philosophy, or the bachelor of letters. Admission standards for students in the Sheffield and Lawrence Scientific Schools were lower than for the B.A. degree, and it took only three rather than the normal four years to complete the degree requirements.

Thus for much of the nineteenth century students in science were not considered full-fledged members of the college communities. Yale, for example, did not permit Sheffield students to sit with regular academic students in Chapel. In 1880, a Yale undergraduate summed up the accepted estimate of Yale's Sheffield Scientific School, which he referred to as "Sheff," by writing that while Yale College was resisting the elective system, "Sheff had long since had well-established and successful elective group courses manned by distinguished scholars, but Sheff did not count, at least not in the affirmative." Fred Lewis Pattee, a student at Dartmouth in the mid 1880s, wrote in later years that the notion of deleting Greek and Latin from the required curriculum struck those in his classrooms "as radical a proposal as would be the removal of the four Gospels from the Biblical canon." "We of the Greek and Latin majority," he remembered, "were inclined to look with high-hat disdain at our own Chandler Scientific School, which was trying, and succeeding, in giving a college education without the classical languages."[6]

When in 1828 Union College adopted a parallel track which allowed the substitution of modern languages for Greek, it was attacked as "the dumping ground of substandard students and scholastic derelicts," just as the Lawrence Scientific School was branded "the resort of shirks and stragglers." For most of the century the bachelor of arts degree remained the property of what was considered the more rigorous and more highly valued classical curriculum. It is not surprising, then, that in 1916 when Columbia College abolished Latin as a requirement for admission it also abolished the bachelor of science degree on the assumption that few would opt for the "meaningless Bachelor of Science degree" if they could now get the bachelor of arts without the classical requirements. A year later President Emeritus Charles William Eliot advocated the same policy for Harvard.[7]

Science was not the only noncanonical field of study to fare badly under this system. History, too, was resisted for many years. As late as 1904, in his inaugural address as president of the University of Wisconsin, Charles Van Hise still sounded a defensive note when he reminded his audience that "no one now doubts the right of pure science to full admission to the list of subjects which may be pursued for a liberal education." "Scarcely less noteworthy," he added, "has been the rise of the great groups of studies classified under political economy, political science, sociology, and history. From a very subordinate, almost insignificant, place in the curriculum they have risen to a place not subordinate to classics or science." Only twenty years earlier, in 1884, Charles William Eliot, president of Harvard, had maintained that "the great majority of American colleges . . . make no requirements in history for admission, and have no teacher of history whatever." The problem was not confined to what Eliot called "inferior colleges," but included such "well-established" institutions as Dartmouth, which had no teacher of history, and Princeton, which had only one, who also taught political science.[8]

Indeed, when Eliot became president in 1869, Harvard's situation was hardly better. Professor Henry W. Torrey, whom Samuel Eliot Morison later characterized as "an excellent representative of the school of dear old gentlemen who taught history as an avocation," was responsible for ancient, medieval, and modern history and American constitutional history, all of which he taught out of textbooks. Eliot rectified the situation by hiring first John Fiske, then Henry Adams, then several of Adams's students including Edward Channing and Albert Bushnell Hart, until Harvard was offering nine or ten courses in American and modern European history by the end of the 1880s. But Eliot was not yet typical.

President James McCosh refused to apologize for the situation at Princeton, insisting that one professor of history was entirely enough: "I think the numerous narrative histories of epochs," McCosh told Eliot, "is just a let-off to easy-going students from the studies which require thought." It was not until 1917 that Eliot could announce with confidence that "the idea of the cultivated person, man or woman, has distinctly changed during the past thirty-five years. . . . The term 'cultivation' is now much more inclusive. It includes elementary knowledge of the sciences, and it ranks high the subjects of history, government, and economics."[9]

Throughout the nineteenth century, the religious and classical bases of the American college came under increasing assault from those who were convinced that American colleges were less and less reflective of the realities of American society. "The present system of collegiate education does not meet the want of the public," President Francis Wayland of Brown University asserted in 1842. "It has been almost impossible in this country, for the merchant, the mechanic, the manufacturer, to educate his son, beyond the course of a common academy unless he gave him the [classical] education preparatory for a profession." The purposes of colleges ought not to be "simply to multiply the number of professional men, whether Lawyers, Physicians, or Divines," but to "be the grand centre of intelligence to all classes and conditions of men, diffusing among all the light of every kind of knowledge." God, he insisted, "intended us for progress, and we counteract his design when we deify antiquity, and bow down and worship an opinion, not because it is either wise or true, but simply because it is ancient." Wayland was one of the first educators to advocate adding modern languages, science, history, political economy, agriculture, law, and the study of education itself to the curriculum and to have sufficient faith in the students' ability to choose according to their needs and the requirements of the world in which they lived. He denied the necessity of a common curriculum for every college: "It would be far better that each should consult the wants of its own locality, and do that best for which it possessed the greatest facilities."[10]

These campaigns to change the patterns of higher education were met with furious counterassaults. It was out of these considerable battles that the modern curriculum was forged. Academic history in the United States, then, has not been a long happy voyage in a stable vessel characterized by blissful consensus about which subjects should form the indisputable curriculum; it has been marked by prolonged and often acrimonious struggle and debate, not very different from that which characterizes the academe in our own day. We should take careful note of the fact that the very curriculum whose alteration so many are lamenting today was itself denounced as trivial, modern, trendy, and anti-intellectual by the defenders of the classical curriculum and was adopted at the turn of the century only over the intense and passionate objections of those who saw in its emergence the end of culture and the decline of civilization.

From the time he assumed the Harvard presidency in 1869, Charles William Eliot's goal was to displace the fixed classical curriculum with a more flexible elective system in which students would be the architects of their own education. "The vulgar argument that the study of the classics is necessary to make a gentleman is beneath contempt," he asserted in 1869. In his famous debate with Princeton President James McCosh in the winter of 1885, Eliot declared that since knowledge had proliferated so markedly, the "presumption" was "against uniformity in education, and in favor of diversity." A university, he insisted, "must try to teach every subject . . . for which there is any demand." A uniform curriculum was by its nature superficial and sacrificed the best scholars to the average. Human beings did not yet possess the wisdom to prescribe which studies "will best develop the human mind in general between the ages of eighteen and twenty-two." Thus a university "while not neglecting the ancient treasures of learning has to keep a watchful eye upon the new fields of discovery, and has to invite its students to walk in new-made as well as in long-trodden paths." The "only hopeful and tenable view," he declared, is that "all branches of sound knowledge are of equal dignity and equal educational value."[11]

McCosh remained unmoved. In his years as president of Princeton, McCosh lost none of the faith he had exhibited in his inaugural address in 1868 when he spoke warmly of "a *classical taste* . . . fostered by living and breathing in the atmosphere of ancient Greece and Rome" without which "our language and literature will run a great risk of hopelessly degenerating." Now he responded to Eliot by warning that he would inform fathers and mothers that their sons were being turned into "mental monstrosities" at a Harvard which offered them "dilettanti courses" in "Music and Art, and French Plays and Novels," instead of rigorous fixed requirements. The "once most illustrious university in America," McCosh declared, "no longer requires its graduates to know the most perfect language, the grandest literature, the most elevated thinking of all antiquity." Everything at Harvard, he complained, "is scattered like the star dust out of which worlds are formed." It was no wonder that at such an institution not only classical learning but religious and moral training were neglected. It was time to spread the news of Harvard's dereliction of duty to the entire world, to inform it "that the college whose motto is *Pro Christo et Ecclesia* teaches no religion to its pupils." McCosh constructed a scenario in which a father exclaimed to Harvard's president: "I sent my son to you believing that man is made in the image of God, you taught him that he is an upper brute, and he has certainly become so; I sent him to you pure, and last night he was carried to my door drunk. Curse ye this college; 'curse ye bitterly.'" Once the public learned of these transgressions, McCosh was convinced, "such an expression of feeling will be called forth, that if we cannot avert the evil in Harvard we may arrest it in the other colleges in the country."[12]

McCosh's was not a lonely voice. President Noah Porter of Yale told the National Education Association in 1877 that "it is vitally important to the culture of this country, . . . to the existence of this country as a country," that the traditional college system and curriculum "should be retained and re-enforced." He simply could not comprehend arguments that modern studies were the equivalent of the ancient. Ancient man, he argued in 1870, was an incomparable being: "decided, clear in his opinions, positive and outspoken in his aims, objective in his life, positive and sharp in his diction, impetuous in his impulses, grand in his connection with the state, heroic in his virtues and almost in his vices. . . . He is always intellectual, impressive, and intelligible, because he is the perfection of the natural and earthly in its purest and noblest man-ifestations." Such a being "enlarges our conception of the forms which humanity may assume." A modern language like English was simply no match for the sublime linguistic creations of the ancients. Like many of his fellow classicists, Porter almost became poetic when discussing classical art "with its outlines as sharply cut as the faces of a crystal, and yet as graceful as the undulations of the moving waters."[13]

In 1884 Andrew West, who several decades later was to engage and defeat Woodrow Wilson in Princeton University's educational wars, asked in the *North American Review,* "Must the Classics Go?" and answered by reaffirming "their immense superiority over all other languages, living or dead, as means of mental discipline." In comparison, English, French, and German were "simply *debris* of the classic languages, mixed with barbaric elements." Shake-speare, after all, had been read by "only a dozen generations. . . . But Homer has already led the way to literary immortality for a hundred generations, with Plato, Virgil, and Horace not far behind." The very fact that modern languages were still *alive,* that is, "growing and hence ever changing . . . unfits them to be a per-manent basis for culture." In 1880 Caleb Mills, professor emeritus of Greek at Wabash College and former Indiana state superinten-dent of education, branded the elective system a "barefaced absur-dity," reminded America that "such men as Webster, Calhoun, Choate . . . did not reach their distinguished eminence, in the palace cars of modern languages and scientific option, now so multitudinous," and prophesied that "the friends of classic learning, sturdy discipline and sterling moral culture" would purge the curriculum "of all incumbent rubbish" and emerge victorious over those who represented "conceit, . . . ignorance, aimless purpose, and inveterate laziness."[14]

Mills and McCosh, of course, were mistaken in their predictions. It was the elective system, not the classical curriculum, that won what Mills called the "irrepressible conflict." Thus after almost a century of battle the traditional classical regimen gave way before a more flexible, more eclectic program characterized by the system of elective courses in which students no longer were held to a single dominant pattern of study but had choices among an ever expanding curriculum and a constantly enlarging canon. The old canon was shattered permanently by the beginning of the twentieth century, but the struggle was far from over.

As implemented by President Eliot at the turn of the century, the elective system required only a single prescribed freshman English course and allowed Harvard students to take whatever combination of courses they desired until they achieved the requisite number for graduation. In this radical form the elective system did not spread widely. Indeed, Eliot's successor, A. Lawrence Lowell, abandoned it as quickly as possible in favor of an elective system featuring concentration and distribution. "We must go forward," he asserted in his 1909 inaugural, "and develop the elective system, making it really systematic." Students' education should not be characterized by either narrow concentration or by the endless sampling of a multitude of subjects. A student ought to be required to study an array of subjects but also to *master* something, "to know in some subject what the ultimate sources of opinion are, and how they are handled by those who profess it. . . . In short, he ought, so far as in him lies, to be both broad and profound."[15] In this form of depth and breadth requirements, of majors and minors, of a separation between the lower and upper divisions of college work, the elective system spread throughout the nation in myriad patterns and is, of course, the system that remains the norm today.

But for many its success never satisfied the hunger for a core to higher education which would touch all students. Though the adherents of the classical curriculum diminished in number and power in the twentieth century, they never disappeared nor completely lost the certainty that theirs was the only sure path to true enlightenment and intellectual order. In Berkeley, Professor Charles Mills Gayley spoke for more than a few of his colleagues when he wrote in 1910 that it was to the abandonment of the classics "with their sweet simplicity and their majesty," that one could attribute "the declining ability to think clearly, to speak and write lucidly, precisely, effectively, the declining love of noble letters and noble art—the declining respect for tradition and authority, for the heritage and the faith—the declining splendour of the ideal. . . . the impoverishment of the age." The strength of the feeling for the lost curriculum can be gauged in Samuel Eliot Morison's 1936 history of Harvard in which Morison's ancestor Charles William Eliot plays an honored role, until Professor Morison unexpectedly exclaims: "It is a hard saying, but Mr. Eliot, more than any other man, is responsible for the greatest educational crime of the century against American youth—depriving him of his classical heritage."[16]

In the same year, President Robert Hutchins of the University of Chicago, in his book *The Higher Learning in America*, advocated a return of the classics. "Correctness in thinking," he asserted, would be achieved only through the medium of a single curriculum designed for the whole people which would be "the same at any time, in any place, under any political, social, or economic conditions." He defended the possibility of such a homogeneous course of study in an argument couched in the syllogistic tone he employed when speaking of education and truth:

> Education implies teaching. Teaching implies knowledge.
> Knowledge is truth. The truth is everywhere the same.
> Hence education should be everywhere the same.

The *only* purpose of education, Hutchins insisted, echoing arguments that had been made since the early nineteenth century, was "the cultivation of the intellect." Therefore, any hint of what he termed "vocationalism," which he defined as "the preparation of men and women for their life work," desecrated the university: "It debases the course of study and the staff. It deprives the university of its only excuse for existence, which is to provide a haven where the search for truth may go on unhampered by utility or pressure for 'results.'" Unfortunately, the United States did not provide fruitful soil for the cultivation of such an education. The problem turned out to be the American people themselves: "The people love money and think that education is a way of getting it. They think too that democracy means that every child should be permitted to acquire the educational insignia that will be helpful in making money. They do not believe in the cultivation of the intellect for its own sake." Hutchins's frustrations stemmed from the fact that his conception of higher education diverged from the spirit of the culture in which he lived. He was convinced that education was debased whenever it wandered from the universal to the specific: "The notion of educating a man to live in any particular time or place, to adjust him to any particular environment, is therefore foreign to a true conception of education." Similarly, he asserted: "Technology as such has no place in general education." The curriculum should be composed principally of what Hutchins called "the permanent studies," which included classical grammar, rhetoric, logic, and mathematics—"chiefly those that use the type of exposition that Euclid employed."

In spite of his admonitions against the practical in education, Hutchins defended the classics on practical as well as ideal grounds, arguing that the classics "are an essential part of general education because it is impossible to understand any subject or to comprehend the contemporary world without them." Like most of his fellow neoclassicists, Hutchins harbored no doubts. There were, he insisted, *no* valid objections to this curriculum. *All* objections stemmed from miseducation: from "the love of money, a

misconception of democracy, a false notion of progress, a distorted idea of utility, and the anti-intellectualism to which all these
lead." Hutchins made it clear that he was writing because higher
education in America was in disorder and needed to achieve the
"real unity" which was possible only through "a hierarchy of
truths which shows us which are fundamental and which sub-
sidiary, which significant and which not." The rational order of
the medieval university had been based upon theology, but since
we were "a faithless generation" we were closer to the Greeks
whose order and discipline were based on metaphysics. The
United States could achieve the same happy state as the Greeks,
through the same means, or so Hutchins's syllogistic reasoning
assured him:

> The aim of higher education is wisdom. Wisdom is knowl-
> edge of principles and causes. Metaphysics deals with the
> highest principles and causes. Therefore metaphysics is the
> highest wisdom.

Again and again it becomes clear in Hutchins's work that his
primary nemesis was less the system of higher education than the
essential nature of American society and culture. If we could learn
from the Greeks and "secure a real university in this country,"
then we might change the character of our civilization and create a
rationally ordered society. "It may be that we can outgrow the
love of money, that we can get a saner conception of democracy,
. . . that we can abandon our false notions of progress and utility
and that we can come to prefer intelligible organization to the
chaos that we mistake for liberty." With this hope, Hutchins
closed his book but not his activities on behalf of turning back the
educational clock.[17]

Those I refer to as neoclassicists were not invariably professional students of the ancient past highly proficient in Greek and
Latin. They were in fact a diverse group ranging in training from
Greek and Latin to the law to political science to English literature. What they shared in common was the belief that education

was an end in itself and not preparation for something else; that proper education consisted of a tightly knit program with a core; that the core had to be composed of "classic" works. With time, the definition of what constituted "the classics" diverged from the nineteenth-century classical curriculum's tight focus on the languages and literature of the ancients to a more general—and amorphous—definition centering upon what J. Winfree Smith called "a book or an essay, whether ancient or modern, or a scientific experiment that is of the utmost excellence in its kind," and what Allan Bloom called, more vaguely, "certain generally recognized classic texts."[18]

Mark Van Doren of Columbia University's English Department joined Hutchins in support of what neoclassicists like to call "liberal education." Liberal studies, he proclaimed in 1943, "are by definition studies which we 'are not at liberty to omit.'" Students should devote their higher education to two principal activities: to learn "the arts of investigation, discussion, criticism, and communication," and to achieve a first-hand acquaintance "with the original books, the unkillable classics, in which these miracles happened." To find this ideal curriculum, Van Doren went back beyond the classical curriculum adopted by the Renaissance humanists to the seven liberal arts of the medieval curriculum: grammar, rhetoric, logic, arithmetic, music, geometry, and astronomy.[19]

As Van Doren's attempt to create still another curricular alternative attests, the problem that plagued the neoclassicists was their inability to agree on precisely what constituted the ideal "liberal" curriculum. Almost a decade earlier, when Hutchins established the Committee on the Liberal Arts at Chicago in 1935 and invited Mortimer Adler, Stringfellow Barr, Scott Buchanan, and Richard McKeon to discuss the liberal arts, the enterprise quickly self-destructed. "McKeon, Adler, and I," Scott Buchanan recalled, "had constructed . . . quite different universes of discourse which reached into deep matters of method and metaphysics. . . . Brought into proximity, the three worlds discharged their energies at each other. Heat and light became thunder and lightning. There was never another general meeting of the whole committee." Although Adler recalled having had more than one meeting, he agreed that the commmittee, in which Hutchins had placed so much hope, "blew apart" because "we could not agree about what books to read or how to read them."[20]

Once again, it was easier to know what to decry than what to construct and members of the committee followed their own paths. Barr and Buchanan took their ideas to St. John's College in Annapolis, Maryland, in 1937 where, as president and dean respectively, they inaugurated a "New Program" intended, in Barr's words, to restore "St. John's to the great and ancient tradition of liberal education." The program, consisting of a general curriculum based upon the Trivium (grammar, rhetoric, logic), the Quadrivium (arithmetic, geometry, music, astronomy), and a series of seminars in which classic books would be discussed, still exists in amended form though it hardly proved to be what Stringfellow Barr had hoped for: "a model for other American colleges to follow," or what Walter Lippmann had predicted: "the seed-bed of the American Renaissance."[21]

Hutchins and Adler, building on the Great Books courses which John Erskine had begun at Columbia University in 1921, established a two-year curriculum at the University of Chicago which married the Great Books idea with an Aristotelian scholasticism that stressed order and hierarchy. "If we can revitalize metaphysics and restore it to its place in the higher learning," Hutchins declared, "we may be able to establish rational order in the modern world as well as in the universities." Ambitious aims like this, which sought to impose order upon society as well as the curriculum, led to doubts about the Great Books enterprise at Chicago and elsewhere. John Erskine complained that some teachers had turned his course in great books

> into a course on philosophy, on some specific philosophy, and others have tried to expand it into an educational method for teaching all subjects. With these aberrations I have no

sympathy whatever. Science, I think, should be studied in the laboratory, not in the literary gropings toward science before laboratories existed; and to confound all the racial and personal variations of history in one philosophy is, I think, to abandon that training of the mind which enables us to observe accurately and make distinctions. I was concerned with no philosophy and no method for a total education; I hoped merely to teach how to read.[22]

In 1952 Hutchins and Adler reached out to the general public by issuing the *Great Books of the Western World* which comprised a 54-volume canon containing 443 works by 74 authors from Homer to Freud. "Until very recently," Hutchins claimed, "these books . . . were the principal instrument of liberal education." In fact, it was not until the demise of the classical curriculum, with its rigorous focus on the Greeks and Romans and on their language more than their literature, that such thinkers as Shakespeare, Milton, Cervantes, Rousseau, Jefferson, Kant, Marx, Darwin, as well as almost all of the other postclassical writers represented in Hutchins's *Great Books of the Western World,* played any significant role in American higher education. Thus what Hutchins portrayed as the historical norm in American education "until very recently" was on the contrary a modern development produced by the very elective system he deplored. Hutchins's nostalgia for an education that never, or at best rarely, existed in the United States, has become a central part of the critique of the American university that exists in our own day. We keep hearing romantic calls for the "restoration" of the classical tradition in a Great Books version that is itself a relatively recent invention. Thus Allan Bloom urged us to turn once more to the wisdom of the past, to "the good old Great Books approach, in which a liberal education means reading certain generally recognized classic texts, just reading them, letting them dictate what the questions are and the method of approaching them—not forcing them into categories we make up, not treating them as historical products, but trying to read them as their authors wished them to be read," though

Bloom never revealed the secret of how we are to ascertain what an author wished.[23]

Undergirding many of the efforts at "restoration" was a profound sense of frustration, anger, and gloom at what the neoclassicists believed the university had become: institutions dominated by science, positivism, and "the vicious specialization of scholarship," as well as by pluralism, "anarchic individualism," the "chaos" of the elective system, and a pragmatic, relativistic definition of truth. Mortimer Adler, who in his long career wrote such manuals as *How to Read a Book* (1940), *How to Think about War and Peace* (1944), *How to Think about God* (1980), and *How to Speak, How to Listen* (1983), was not reticent in identifying the problem. Democracy, he told the Conference on Science, Philosophy, and Religion in September, 1940, was in greater peril "from the mentality of its teachers than from the nihilism of Hitler. It is the same nihilism in both cases, but Hitler's is more honest and consistent, less blurred by subtleties and queasy qualifications, and hence less dangerous." A month later, manifesting the same distrust of students that pervades our own time, he asked: "What, then, is the difference between our youth and Hitler's? Even if ours have not read *Mein Kampf* . . . they have become 'realists' of the same sort, believing only in the tangible rewards of success—money, fame, and power."[24]

Referring to the "glorious, Quixotic failure of President Hutchins to accomplish any of the essential reforms which American education so badly needs," Adler asked: "Can anything be done about American education?" His answer—"I doubt it"—was emblematic of the ultimate failure of those who sought a return to the traditional and exclusive system that once governed American colleges.[25]

Looking Eastward:
The Career of Western Civ

It was not the neoclassicists who filled the vacuum many perceived after the demise of the classical curriculum. That distinction went to a group of educators during World War I who, with the encouragement of a federal government anxious to help Americans understand why after almost two centuries they were turning once again to Europe, devised new general education courses soon to bear the name Western Civilization, or in the college vernacular, Western Civ.

The historian Daniel Boorstin has depicted the First World War as a watershed for American conceptions of Europe. Prior to the war Americans tended to see their country as "a kind of non-Europe." The designations "American" and "European," he maintains, were used less as geographical terms than as "logical antitheses." Europe "was a handy mirror in which to see what we were not, and hence to help us discover what we were." Certainly European history courses existed before 1914—in Berkeley, University of California freshmen could take History 1 which covered "the progress of western European civilization from prehistoric times to the completion of the Panama Canal"—but the war brought such courses new meaning. Irwin Edman, a sophomore

at Columbia College in 1914, remembered how the European
conflict made Professor Carlton Hayes's course on Europe since
1815 increasingly popular with undergraduates: "Up to the autumn
of 1914 Europe seemed to most American college students a solar
system away." The war changed all of this. "European history
ceased to be the anthropology and archaeology of distant peoples
who spoke remote languages. It became as alive as yesterday's
events; it was what explained today's news."[1]

Indeed, in a sense Western Civilization courses did grow out of
this desire to explain "today's news." After the United States
entered the war, the federal government's Committee on Education and Special Training established the Student Army Training
Corps (SATC) on campuses throughout the nation and requested
the host colleges to create an interdisciplinary War Issues Course
explaining the underlying and immediate causes of the war.
Although propagandistic motives were denied by everyone concerned, the courses inevitably reflected the Wilsonian notion that
the war was a struggle between Enlightenment and Barbarism,
between the principles and practices of democracy and those of
autocracy, with the future of civilization hanging in the balance.
At the University of Michigan, for example, Professor Claude Van
Tyne gave a series of lectures on Germany with such titles as,
"How Autocracy Drills Its Subjects," "Dreams of World Power,"
"Superman," and "A State Without Moral Obligations," while
Professor Edward R. Turner taught his students that "the English,
more than any other people in the world, except the French and
ourselves . . . have the humanitarian spirit, a desire for fair play and
to do what is right, to help people who are weaker than themselves, not to take advantage of weaker people, in other words to
do to others as they would be done by." The Germans, on the
other hand, "carry on war as they have in France and Belgium
because the German people do not have the humanitarian spirit of
fair play, which the English, American and French do have."
Albert Kerr Heckel, Dean of Lafayette College, wrote that "we
were advised not to make the course one of propaganda, and yet it

could not escape being propaganda." The purpose of the course, he felt, should be to "tell the ugly truth about Germany" by explaining how the "dominant democratic ideal among European peoples in general" had "failed with the Teuton," and exploring "what is wrong with Germany . . . the defects of German character . . . the falsity of her political creed and her philosophy of might." Never before, he concluded, "have we felt more definitely that there are moral forces at work in history making. And as a result it may be that the teacher of history will, for at least a time, be also something of an advocate." The Committee on Education and Special Training made it clear that the purpose of the course was "to enhance the morale of the members of the corps by giving them an understanding of what the war is about and of the supreme importance to civilization of the cause for which we are fighting."[2]

The course was so successful at Columbia College that its director, Dean F. J. E. Woodbridge, began to consider it a potential foundation for a course "which will give the generations to come a common background of ideas and commonly understood standards of judgment." Thus at Columbia the War Issues Course became not an end but a beginning. It was followed by a Peace Issues Course and ultimately in the fall of 1919 by a required freshman course, Contemporary Civilization, which surveyed the development of Western Civilization and familiarized students with contemporary world problems. Ten years later, a second year of Contemporary Civilization was prescribed for sophomores. As Carol Gruber has shown, CC, as it quickly became known, manifested its wartime origins and continued to serve patriotic purposes. One of its founders, Dean Herbert E. Hawkes, maintained that it was intended to thwart the "destructive element in our society" by equipping students to "meet the arguments of the opponents of decency and sound government" and make the college student a "citizen who shall be safe for democracy." Since this course was so instrumental in the establishment of Western Civ as the norm across the nation, it is worth noting that it came into being with a significant amount of political and ideological content both during and after World War I.[3]

The urges that established Western Civ as the core liberal arts course included more than the patriotism of the moment. For a decade or more before the war, Columbia and many other American colleges were perplexed: what would, what should replace classics as the core of undergraduate education? "The college," declared President Jacob Gould Schurman of Cornell in 1907, "is without clear-cut notions of what a liberal education is and how it is to be secured." This "paralysis," Schurman insisted, affected "every college of arts in America."[4]

The happy discovery professors made on a number of campuses during the war was that the immediate needs of the federal government coincided with several long-term educational demands. Even before World War I a few U.S. historians had been looking for ways to place American history in greater perspective. The Committee of Seven, appointed by the American Historical Association to study the teaching of history in the secondary schools, argued in its 1899 report that the history of the United States taught by itself was, in the words of Professor Lucy M. Salmon, "insufficient. It gives but a warped, narrow, circumscribed view of history, —it is history detached from its natural foundation— European history, it is history suspended in mid-air."[5] This conviction won a wider audience with the advent of global wars on either side of a worldwide depression, shared experiences which certainly nurtured feelings of connection with Europe that had not been characteristic of nineteenth-century Americans. These events prompted Americans to look eastward, back toward Europe, with an intensity they had not experienced for most of their national history and promoted a feeling of belonging to a "Western" civilization.

It would be a mistake to attribute the attraction of Western Civ primarily to international factors. There were important domestic forces at work as well. At a time when ethnic diversity bore heavily on American consciousness because of the massive immigration

from Southern and Eastern Europe, the migrations of African
Americans from the South to the cities of the North, and the
European war which exacerbated tensions between ethnic groups
in the United States and gave rise to President Wilson's warnings
about "hyphenated" Americans, the advent of Western Civ
promised to be a unifying and assimilative force which taught the
separate groups that they had a common and deeply rooted heritage that bound them together. Columbia University's president,
Nicholas Murray Butler, who complained that the elective system
had destroyed "that common body of knowledge which held educated men together in understanding and in sympathy" for more
than a thousand years, hailed the advent of the Contemporary
Civilization course as a worthy substitute which would serve as "a
unifying force of common understanding, common appreciation
and common sentiment." As the historian Carolyn Lougee has
put it, "In cultural terms, the Western Civ ideal was homogenizing and normative: it socialized the young from whatever particularist background traditions to a uniform standard of thinking and
behaving that ought to characterize America's expanding educated class."[6]

It performed the same function *within* the colleges themselves.
The elimination first of Greek and then of Latin as entrance
requirements increased the number of public high school graduates at elite schools like Columbia which meant, as Lionel Trilling
later observed, a considerable increase in the number of students
who "came from ethnic and social groups not formerly represented in the College." Dean Herbert Hawkes complained in 1918
that too many students now lived at home, attended college from
nine to five, and regarded it primarily as a means to further their
careers: "They have no use for college affairs and regard Columbia
less as an Alma Mater than as an Efficiens Pater." Dean Frederick
Keppel broached the issue more frankly, noting in 1914, "One of
the commonest references that one hears with regard to Columbia is that its position at the gateway of European immigration
makes it socially uninviting to students who come from homes of

refinement. The form which the inquiry takes in these days of slowly-dying race prejudice is, 'Isn't Columbia overrun with European Jews who are most unpleasant persons socially?'" Lionel Trilling surmised that the problem of diminishing social homogeneity and unity was behind Columbia's restoration of football in 1915, after a decade of banishment, in "an effort to create the sense of collegiate solidarity among the students." From the point of view of Trilling and many of his colleagues, the introduction of Western Civ was a more satisfactory means to the same end. Clearly, the shaping of the college curriculum in response to an increasingly diverse population has not been confined to our own time.[7]

The Western Civ courses that evolved on campus after campus in these years went beyond the immediate, practical connections to Europe and envisioned the United States and Europe tied together in a cultural embrace that had its historical origins in the classical world and its development in medieval, Renaissance, and modern Europe. It was a Whiggish view of history that pictured "Western Civilization" as the end product of all of world history, or at least all of world history that *mattered*, since entire continents, whole peoples, and complete historical epochs were ignored as if they had not existed, and for the purposes of the new Western Civ ethos, they hadn't. Justus Buchler, a professor of philosophy at Columbia University, made—and defended—the point that as taught at Columbia, one must always qualify the term "Contemporary Civilization" with the phrase "in the West." This limitation, Buchler explained, stemmed "not from dim awareness of the Orient . . . nor from perversity and false cultural pride, but because Western society is the society of Western students, and because the number of available men versed in Eastern culture has always been lamentably small." It is not inappropriate to note that such scholars were "lamentably" few largely *because* "civilization" as understood and taught in twentieth-century American colleges invariably carried the adjective "Western," whether it was articulated or not. It is also instructive to recognize that Buchler viewed the world as a simple polarity between the "Orient" and the "Occident," and felt no need to mention Africa, in spite of America's substantial demographic and cultural connections to that continent. James Harvey Robinson, whose European history textbooks were deeply influential in shaping the nature of Western Civ courses, was similarly open about the process of inclusion. In *The Ordeal of Civilization* (1926), he revealed that in making "a fresh selection from the records of the past," he decided that "only those considerations would properly find a place which clearly served to forward the main purpose of seeing more and more distinctly how this, our present Western civilization . . . has come about."[8]

World War I stimulated not only a change in the university curriculum but in American thought. And it must be stressed how rapid and marked this change was. Nineteenth-century Americans did not tend to conceive of themselves as participants in a common Western civilization. They were, in fact, deeply ambivalent about European culture. On the one hand, many Americans, especially among the elite, lived in the shadow of European culture and never felt as independent culturally as they did politically and economically. They suffered acutely from such charges as those leveled by the Reverend Sydney Smith in the *Edinburgh Review* in 1820 when he asked, "In the four quarters of the globe, who reads an American book? or goes to an American play? or looks at an American picture or statue?" And they agreed with Henry James's litany of American deficiencies: "no cathedrals, nor abbeys, nor little Norman churches; no great Universities nor public schools—no Oxford, nor Eton, nor Harrow; no literature, no novels, no museums, no pictures."[9]

On the other hand, Americans remained deeply suspicious of Europe, its institutions, and its culture. In 1825 John Adams warned Thomas Jefferson against importing European tutors and professors for the new University of Virginia: "The Europeans are all deeply tainted with prejudices, both ecclesiastical and temporal, which they can never get rid of." Jefferson himself did not look on in satisfaction at the prospect of immigrants from Europe bringing to America the fruits of a common civilization. On the contrary, he worried that the mass of European immigrants, coming as they did from very different and much more restrictive governmental systems, would fail to appreciate the principles inherent in the American constitutions which, Jefferson insisted, "are more peculiar than those of any other in the universe," but instead would "bring with them the principles of the governments they leave. . . . These principles, with their language, they will transmit to their children." The result would "warp and bias" the American system and "render it a heterogeneous, incoherent, distracted mass." "I hope," Jefferson declared on another occasion, "we may find some means of shielding ourselves from foreign influence—political, commercial, or in what form attempted. I can scarcely withhold myself from joining in the wish of Silas Dean, that there were an ocean of fire between this and the old world!" The future president James Buchanan agreed when he insisted in 1815 that "we ought to drive from our shores foreign influence, and cherish exclusively American feelings. Foreign influence has been in every age, the curse of republics." It would be better, Secretary of War William Crawford declared in 1816, "to incorporate, by a human and benevolent policy, the natives of our forests in the great American family of freedom, than to receive, with open arms, the fugitives of the old world, whether their flight has been the effect of their crimes or their virtues." Similarly, in 1818, Secretary of State John Quincy Adams, in discussing European immigration, did not open his arms to embrace unconditionally fellow inhabitants of a shared Western Civilization, but rather warned future migrants from Europe that "They must cast off the European skin never to resume it. They must look forward to their posterity rather than backward to their ancestors." "I must walk toward Oregon, and not toward Europe," Henry David Thoreau proclaimed. ". . . The Atlantic is a Lethean stream, in our passage over which we have had an opportunity to forget the Old World and its institutions."

Those "persons, books, manners, etc.," which were appropriate for European lands, Walt Whitman announced in 1871, "are but exiles and exotics here." Sixteen years earlier, in the first edition of his *Leaves of Grass,* Whitman spoke for many of his fellow Americans when he sang of his cultural distinctiveness:

> *I too am not a bit tamed. . . . I too am untranslatable,*
> *I sound my barbaric yawp over the roofs of the world.*[10]

The literary scholar Werner Sollors, after surveying what he terms American "ethnic literature" from Hector St. John Crève-coeur's *Letters from an American Farmer* in 1782 to Ole Rolvaag's novel *Giants in the Earth* in 1927, concluded that "America appears as the 'un-Europe'" depicted as "the land without kings, bishops, or medieval castles," and characterized by "suggestive images of exodus and deliverance, newness and rebirth." When, toward the end of the nineteenth century, the historian Herbert Baxter Adams proposed that American democracy had been imported as germs from Teutonic tribal practices, his student Frederick Jackson Turner, in the famous paper he delivered at the Columbian Exposition of 1893, repudiated this external explanation of American politics and society in good nineteenth-century fashion by looking inward and focusing upon the American frontier as the mechanism which molded the culture and character of the United States whose citizens were "a mixed race, English in neither nationality nor characteristics." Indeed, the "West" that most engaged the imagination of nineteenth-century Americans referred not to Europe but to the successive American frontiers stretching westward from the Eastern seaboard and progressively away from the Old World.[11]

Turner's notions of the indigenous nature of American identity certainly lived on well into the twentieth century, but increasingly they shared space, somewhat uneasily, with the assertions of historians like Carlton J. H. Hayes of Columbia University who taught his students and the many readers of his widely used 1932 textbook that for more than two thousand years "Europe has been the seat of that continuous high civilization which we call 'western,' —which has come to be the distinctive civilization of the American continents as well as of Europe." Hayes's pronouncement reflects the centrality of the Western Civilization idea in the years between the world wars which saw the introduction of Western Civ courses in colleges throughout the nation. Western Civ shared with such other components of the General Education movement of the interwar years as the Great Books courses a sense of universal validity. General education, President Henry M. Wriston of Lawrence College insisted in 1934, was "an education useful to all who possess it, at all times, and under all circumstances." It was precisely this claim that was to become suspect to increasing numbers of students and faculty in the coming decades.[12]

Although Western Civ remained dominant in the years immediately following the Second World War, and even penetrated such new territory as the University of Chicago, its momentum soon ebbed. As Gilbert Allardyce has argued persuasively, postwar developments were simply not conducive to its continued primacy. The struggle with the Soviet Union for technological superiority heightened America's awareness of the increased need for specialized knowledge. The decline of colonialism and the growing recognition of the existence and importance of the Third World taught Americans that the world they lived in consisted of diverse cultures and peoples who could neither be understood nor explained through the concepts at the center of the Western Civ course. Domestic developments which saw the emergence of minority peoples and power in the United States and the increased presence on campuses of students and faculty from minority groups, including those from Eastern and Southern European immigrant cultures, reminded the nation of the diversity at the center of our own history which could not be comprehended solely through tracing the development of Western and Northern European civilization.[13]

A more anthropological and comprehensive way of perceiving culture also undermined the Western Civ curriculum with its evolutionary and hierarchical predispositions. During a 1976 American Historical Association session on the Western Civ survey, Frederic L. Cheyette of Amherst College articulated the growing skepticism when he argued that despite its claims to universality, the Western Civ curriculum was "truncated and provincial: its culture was essentially political and philosophical, nodding occasionally towards science, less often towards poetry. It dismissed the visual arts with a slide show and ignored music completely, as though on some absolute ontological scale Mozart had been weighed against Voltaire and found wanting. Popular culture, of course, was beneath notice."[14]

Although it declined, Western Civ did not die in those years after World War II; it lived—and lives—on in a bewildering array of forms. I took and later taught a two-semester Western Civ course first as a freshman and then as a young instructor at the City College of New York in the 1950s, just as students throughout the country were—and still are—taking such courses. What died, or at least began a precipitous decline, was a certain set of assumptions that had surrounded Western Civ from its inception and had given it, for a short time, an unparalleled position of privilege in the humanities and the university. What died, or at least suffered an inexorable blow, was a certain arrogance, an unquestioned assurance that Western Civilization embodied *all* the culture and history and literature we needed to know to live our lives and comprehend our past and present.

It is important to recognize that the Western Civilization survey course, which many critics of the contemporary university imply has long constituted the heart and soul of the humanities curriculum and therefore must be defended to the death, did not come into being until somewhere around the First World War and remained in the ascendancy for less than fifty years before fading from prominence in the decades after the Second World War. The complexity of knowledge, the complexity of culture, the complexity of the world, and the complexity of the United States itself became more difficult and more dangerous to deny and more imperative to confront and comprehend. All of these developments created an atmosphere less supportive to ideas of a unified core curriculum devoted to promulgating the dominance of a single cultural stream that would explain the United States to its people, whether that curriculum was dominated by classics or by Western Civ. The appealingly simple syllogistic universe and solutions of Robert Hutchins and his colleagues appeared less and less credible.

Almost everywhere in the post–World War II university world, colleges took a second and far more critical look at their general education programs and core courses. Although Harvard issued its famous 1945 report, *General Education in a Free Society,* which recommended that all students be required to take a course in "Great Texts of Literature" and another course in "Western Thought and Institutions," the objective of which would be "an examination of the institutional and theoretical aspects of the Western heritage," the faculty adopted so many options to the report's recommended core curriculum that it began to resemble the very elective system it was meant to modify. During the 1949 debate on the report's proposed Western Civ course, which was modeled on Columbia's Contemporary Civilization course, faculty critics insisted that the stress on *Western* thought and institutions embodied a myopic and limited view of the modern world, perpetuated the myth of civilization as a monopoly of those countries bordering the Atlantic Ocean, and ignored the virtues of comparing the values and institutions of Western societies with those of other cultures.[15]

In 1968, the year before Stanford University's History of Western Civilization course, which had been initiated as a prescribed course for all freshmen in 1935, was dropped as a requirement, its director, Paul S. Seaver, admitted that "many of us as faculty are no longer convinced that there is a standard or specifiable body of knowledge or information necessary for a liberal education." The crucial function "of introducing historical concepts, modes of analysis, etc.," he concluded, "is common to all history courses and does not, therefore, require the setting of a Western Civ survey." The authors of the multivolume report, *The Study of Education at Stanford* (1968), agreed. "General education, as epitomized by the Chicago curriculum of the Hutchins era and the Columbia two-year sequences in Humanities and Contemporary Civilization," they observed, "is dead or dying." Why, they asked, "is it more important for a student to learn some calculus than some economics? Are we really sure that mastery of a foreign language is more important than mastery of one of the fine arts?" Rather than a series of inflexible, prescribed requirements, representing "a set of political compromises among interest groups in the faculty," they called for "a new kind of general education" based upon the understanding that "the University cannot in any event impress upon its students the total content of present knowledge, and [that] it is impossible to choose what exactly it is that every student should know without imposing arbitrary constraints on the range of free inquiry." Thus instead of teaching overviews of their field as a whole, professors should be permitted to cover those aspects about which they knew and cared most deeply: "the Intellectual History of Europe in the Nineteenth Century rather than the History of Western Civilization, . . . Organizational Behavior rather than Introduction to Sociology." Students should be given the freedom "to discover new interests . . . and to explore the many fields and endeavors" open to them. "From this common freedom," the report concluded, "may emerge a form of general education far better suited to the characteristics of a university than that to which we pay lip service now."[16]

Four years later, the Carnegie Commission on Higher Education criticized Western Civilization programs for covering too much and exploring too little in depth and recommended dropping the term *general education* "because it carries with it connotations of past efforts at a general coverage of all essential knowledge. Such coverage has proved impossible, despite repeated experiments over the past 70 years. 'Essential knowledge' no longer has the intellectual (classical) and/or theological core that once allowed a student to cover it all in one college career." Instead of the "preselected content" of general education programs, the commission stressed both process—emphasis should be placed "on cultivation of curiosity, on development of critical ability, on wider perspectives on self and on cultures, on ways to approach knowledge"—and relevance: the curriculum should have a direct relationship to the students for whom it is intended and the times in which it is taught.[17] There was certainly nothing particularly new or revolutionary about these proposals; Charles William Eliot might have been heard whispering "Amen!"

At Columbia University itself, the famous CC course, which had served as a model for so many Western Civ courses, was severely diluted. In 1959 the second year of the CC requirement was discontinued, and in 1968 its common source book—which had constituted the very heart of the course for over two decades and had been regarded "by staff and students alike, as one of the most valuable features of the course"—was abandoned for paperbacks chosen by faculty. When the Columbia College faculty met to consider Daniel Bell's report on reforming general education in 1964, they opted to do absolutely nothing. "From my long experience of the College," Lionel Trilling reported, "I can recall no meetings on an educational topic that were so poorly attended and so lacking in vivacity. . . . Through some persuasion of the *Zeitgeist*, the majority of the faculty were no longer concerned with general education."[18]

Trilling was entirely correct. The diminution of Western Civ courses and general education programs, like their adoption earlier in this century, were caused not by willful groups of malcontents and philistines, who somehow seized power, but by deep societal changes and developments—by alterations in the *Zeitgeist*. College curricula do not exist apart from the culture in which they develop; they are products of that culture and both reflect and influence it. Thus, significant curricular changes are invariably and

inextricably linked to significant changes in the general society and
culture. The reasons behind the transformation of the classical
college curriculum into the modern system of electives at the end
of the last century and the rapid decline of Western Civ more
recently illustrate this truth. Unfortunately, it's a truth that has
not penetrated our consciousness deeply enough. The recent con-
tinuation of the clash over the Western Civ curriculum at Stanford
University serves as an excellent example of the distortions that
remain in our thinking about higher education.

In February 1988, *Newsweek* printed a full-color reproduction
of David's famous *Death of Socrates* depicting the ancient Greek
philosopher, surrounded by grieving students, as he is about to
swallow a cup of poison hemlock. David's painting was used to
illustrate *Newsweek*'s report of a curriculum debate at Stanford
University entitled, "Say Goodnight Socrates: Stanford University
and the Decline of the West." The use of death as a metaphor
for the state of Western Civilization, and the tendency to equate
the college courses entitled Western Civilization with Western
culture itself, were not unusual. Stanford, the *San Francisco
Chronicle* proclaimed in large headlines, "Puts an End to Western
Civilization."[19]

Secretary of Education William Bennett referred to the re-
consideration of the introductory course that was going on at
Stanford as "curricular debasement" and declared that Stanford's
proposed new course would "trash Shakespeare and Plato." In a
speech to educators he complained that "nonsense is driving out
sense on our campuses" and charged that the "trendy light-
weights" who were responsible for eliminating classic works from
the curriculum and replacing them with "dopiness and trivialities"
were influenced less by Karl Marx than by "Groucho Marx—in
collaboration with Daffy Duck." Ultimately Bennett visited the
campus in order to denounce the curricular changes in person,
and debated Stanford President Donald Kennedy on national television. We must "study, nurture, and defend the West," Bennett
proclaimed at Stanford, because the West "is good."[20]

The occasion for all of this fervor was an internal academic discussion at Stanford over the freshman introductory course. As we have seen, Stanford abolished its required Western Civilization course for entering students in 1969. By the mid-1970s some Stanford faculty began to lobby for the restoration of a core freshman requirement, and in 1980 Stanford instituted a year-long Western Culture course consisting of a number of different "tracks" among which entering students could choose, depending on their interests and intended majors. Since the tracks adopted diverse readings to accomplish their separate goals, a compact collective list of about fifteen books was chosen to provide the students with a shared background. For the ancient world, selections from the Old and New Testaments, Plato, Homer, and a Greek tragedy were included. For the Middle Ages and Renaissance the readings were from Saint Augustine, Thomas More, Machiavelli, Luther, and Galileo. The modern world was represented by Voltaire, Marx and Engels, Freud, and Darwin. The stated purpose of the short list of readings was to ensure a "common intellectual experience" rather than to provide a sacred canon of indispensable texts.[21]

From the beginning, there were Stanford faculty who found the core list hopelessly parochial: too few books were from the modern period—only four representing the last four hundred years. Although the course was being taught to American students, the list contained nothing from the United States or the entire Western Hemisphere. Even within the European context, too many peoples were totally ignored—the cultures of Russia and Eastern Europe, Scandinavia, Spain and Portugal. The course concentrated on authors and texts rather than issues and problems, which lent itself to the intended or unintended creation of an inalterable canon excluding the "other" and completely ignoring the cultures of everyday life. Faculty opposition was not to Western culture but to the narrow geographical, aesthetic, and intellectual ways in which that culture was construed and represented.

One result of this disagreement was that from the start a considerable number of professors, especially among the younger, minority, and female faculty, hesitated to teach the course. When Mary Louise Pratt, an Assistant Professor of Spanish and Portuguese, was asked to participate, she declined because of "the absence of the Iberian world and the Americas from the core list." Another result was the ongoing revisions faculty made as they taught the course. As one Stanford professor put it, "nearly all tracks, it turned out, were somewhat cavalier in their commitment to the core list." Barry Katz who taught the Values, Technology, Science, and Society track testified that for years he was puzzled about how to fit St. Augustine into the course. More than a few professors made their own alterations, adding, for example, women writers like Sappho or African American writers like Frederick Douglass to the core list.[22]

Though the core list was often altered and regularly ignored, its very existence led to protests from African American, Hispanic, Native American, Asian American, and women's organizations. "We're not trying to get rid of the Great Books," William King, president of Stanford's Black Student Union declared. "But these men didn't write and think in a vacuum. When I got to Stanford, I thought I'd be hearing about the influence of the Egyptians on the Greeks, and how the Islamic world contributed to the Western understanding of medicine and mathematics." The issue, King told the Faculty Senate, "is not the destruction or preservation of Western history," but "the acknowledgment that the West as we know it is not European but international in its origin and tradition." Dean Carolyn Lougee asked the Senate to consider whether "the Western Civ course that had served American universities so well for so long, is adequate to the new political exigencies, the new social realities, and new scholarly understandings" and whether "a new model of a shared freshman culture course needs to be invented to serve the more diversified population that is now on our campus and in the country's future."[23]

By 1986 these challenges prompted Stanford to review the Western Culture course and, after two years of widespread discussion and what the chair of the Faculty Senate characterized as "the longest, most thoughtful debate in the Senate's history," to recommend a substitute requirement called Culture, Ideas, Values— whose acronym, not coincidentally, was CIV. Whether it was intended or not, this shift in title reflected the shift in interest from a focus on *Western* civilization to a more catholic interest in civilization and culture in their larger sense. Inaugurated in the Fall of 1989, CIV kept most of the older tracks, but in place of a fixed core reading list, common texts or authors would be chosen each year by the faculty teaching the course. The core list for 1989 consisted of the Bible, Plato, St. Augustine, Machiavelli, Rousseau, and Marx. In addition, each track had to include "the study of works by women, minorities, and persons of color," and had to examine "at least one of the non-European cultures that have become components of our diverse American society." Although ample scope was given to increase the modern components of the course, all tracks were required to "include treatment of ancient and medieval cultures," though they didn't necessarily have to be Western ancient and medieval cultures.

The guidelines certainly allowed for courses that were relatively similar to those taught under the older curriculum and, in fact, these more traditional European-centered courses continued to predominate, enrolling about 90 percent of all entering freshmen. In 1992 the historian Judith C. Brown enumerated the requirements for the 345 students in her History 1. In addition to a textbook entitled *The Western Heritage,* the students

> are required to read substantial segments of Aristotle's *Politics,* portions of the Old and New Testaments, the *Aeneid,* parts of Josephus' *History of the Jewish Wars* as well as of Augustine's *Confessions* and *City of God;* parts of the *Koran,* the *Hadith,* and Thomas Aquinas' *Summa Theologica,* as well as Maimonides' *Guide for the Perplexed* and al-Ghazali's

Deliverance from Error; they read most of Dante's *Inferno* and large segments of the *Lais* of Marie de France, Boccaccio's *Decameron,* and Chaucer's *Canterbury Tales;* they also read much of Christine de Pizan's *City of Ladies,* Castiglione's *The Courtier,* Bernal Diaz's *Account of the Conquest of Mexico,* and Aztec accounts of the same event; Machiavelli's *Prince* and More's *Utopia* are read in their entirety. . . . This covers most, but not all, of our reading for the fall term. The students then go on to equally demanding readings in History 2 and 3, which are part of the freshman requirement and which cover the Reformation to the present.

Clearly, CIV embodied the Committee on Undergraduate Studies' call for "evolution, not revolution." If Allan Bloom and Jesse Jackson "were both to pore over the reading lists for the CIV courses," Raoul Mowatt, a Stanford undergraduate, observed, "Bloom would have cause for a much greater degree of satisfaction."[24]

Nevertheless, the guidelines also permitted such experimental new courses as one called "Europe and the Americas" which focused on the interaction of European, African, and Native American cultures in the Americas. Its reading list included canonical European texts, as well as American, Caribbean, Latin American, and Native American texts. For example, Shakespeare's *The Tempest* was examined alongside Aimé Césaire's *A Tempest,* José Enrique Rodó's *Ariel,* and Roberto Fernández Retamar's *Caliban.* This method of juxtaposing European and New World texts was introduced by the Stanford anthropologist Renato Rosaldo who testified that when he assigned Augustine's *Confessions* along with *Old Man Hat,* the life history of a Navajo man, "both texts got better." George Dekker of Stanford's English Department agreed: "I cannot conceive of a student who will not be wiser for reading in Richard Wright's *Black Boy* about growing up colored in Mississippi or for reading Plato's *Apology* about Socrates, as an old man in fifth century (B.C.) Athens, facing a choice between death and renunciation of his beliefs. The one experience . . . illuminates the other, and all of our students should be familiar with both."

These were the developments that led Secretary Bennett, *Newsweek,* the *San Francisco Chronicle,* and many other individuals, newspapers, and magazines to proclaim the demise of Socrates and the end of Western Civilization. A great university, Bennett charged, "was brought low by the very forces which modern universities came into being to oppose—ignorance, irrationality and intimidation." The Stanford faculty, Dinesh D'Souza asserted, "have placed ideological prejudice at the center of their curriculum."[25]

The attack on Stanford's curriculum, like the attack on contemporary universities in general, is disturbing precisely because it demonstrates such a shallow and uninformed view of our history. The Western Civ curriculum, portrayed by conservative critics of the university in our time as apolitical and of extremely long duration, was in fact neither. It was a twentieth-century phenomenon which had its origins in a wartime government initiative, and its heyday lasted for scarcely fifty years. Its decline as the dominant feature of the humanities curriculum was brought about by alterations in the spirit and temper of the times, not by the infusion of handfuls of 1960s radicals into the faculties of the 1970s and 1980s, as critics of the contemporary university assert *ad nauseam.*

As this and the preceding chapters have demonstrated, to overturn a well-entrenched educational system takes more than a handful of radicals. Educators like George Ticknor of Harvard and Francis Wayland of Brown had attempted to change the system fundamentally in the early decades of the nineteenth century and failed; their ideas prevailed only in the more amenable environment of the postbellum industrial state. As the United States became an urban, industrial state the need for increased numbers of people with specialized linguistic, scientific, engineering, and social science skills grew, and universities responded to these needs, most frequently against the resolute opposition of traditionalists who perceived fundamental change as desecration. And even then the changes came gradually and were often accepted reluctantly and at a great personal price. Although President Barnard helped to build Columbia College into a modern university, he demonstrated the pressures basic change exerts by remarking in 1873: "If the final outcome of all the boastful discoveries of modern science is to disclose to men that they are more evanescent than the shadow of the swallow's wing upon the lake . . . give me, then, I pray, no more science. I will live on in my simple ignorance as my fathers did before me."[26]

Educational reform has come no more rapidly or easily in this century. The changes that engulfed nineteenth- and twentieth-century higher education were not concocted in some ivory tower version of the smoke-filled room by the academic equivalents of calculating political bosses: they resulted from fundamental cultural and material transformations and were related to the needs of the people and the society.

English and American:
A Tale of Two Literatures

The story of the reception and inclusion of English and American literatures into university life constitutes a fascinating episode in the history of curriculum reform. It is a story that may surprise some; it should temper others who make easy and insubstantial claims about the history and status of the texts we think of as canonical.

In his 1990 book *The Death of Literature,* Alvin Kernan complained that "what were once the masterpieces of literature, the plays of Shakespeare or the novels of Flaubert, are now void of meaning, or, what comes to the same thing, filled with an infinity of meanings." No longer, he lamented, was literature conceived of as "the near-sacred myths of human experience of the world and the self, the most prized possessions of culture, universal statements about an unchanging and essential human nature."[1]

What is notable about Kernan's approach is his insistence that the canon in which Shakespeare and Flaubert were imperishable fixtures, whose meaning was "inherent in the text . . . [and] set in place for all time by the writer's word craft," has been disrupted primarily in our own time in which "Marxists fight feminists for the right to identify the smells arising from the literary corpse."

Literature's "prosperity and its social usefulness rely on a group of poems, plays, novels that are by general agreement not only its principal stock in trade but its accumulated capital as well. Give away, lose, or discredit these texts—Homer, Shakespeare, Balzac —and literature is out of business." And that is precisely what has happened: "The great historical tradition extending from Homer to the present has been broken. . . . The literary canon has been analyzed and disintegrated, while literary history itself has been discarded."[2]

The apocalyptic tone of Kernan's requiem is not uncommon. Harold Bloom, in an interview on the eve of the publication of his *The Western Canon* (1994), announced: "I fully believe that before I am dead of old age [he was sixty-four at the time], we're not going to have departments of English or literature. A lot of them already are being named departments of cultural studies, and are doing Batman comics and theme parks and all sorts of *hazare* [junk, garbage], to use the grand old Yiddish word for it." "What I hope for," he added in a whisper, "is some saving remnant. I just hope that, on the model of what are called classics departments, that there can be groups of six or seven women and men who want to study literature and teach literature." And then he concluded with a sigh: "But I suppose this may be vain hope on my part." His book itself opens with a chapter called "An Elegy for the Canon" and ends with an "Elegiac Conclusion." The elegies are occasioned by Bloom's conviction that "nothing ever will be the same because . . . [we] cannot be certain that fresh generations will rise up to prefer Shakespeare and Dante to all other writers. The shadows lengthen in our evening land, and we approach the second millennium expecting further shadowing." All of this gloom should prod us to look more closely into the nature and the history of the literary canon that is being mourned so fervently.[3]

A canon, of course, is composed not merely of subject matter but of attitudes toward and ways of approaching that subject matter. In nineteenth-century American colleges the classics were valued less as literature than as language—repositories of grammatical and syntactical structures which, the Yale Report insisted, employed "every faculty of the mind . . . the memory, judgment, and reasoning powers." In 1854 President John Maclean of Princeton coupled the teaching of the classics to the inculcation of "mental discipline." Eight years earlier, as vice president, Maclean had demanded an explanation when he learned that Professor Evert Topping was teaching Greek literature in addition to the Greek language. Topping insisted that he employed literature to engage the students' interest and end the tedium of parsing and translation that often caused his classes to be interrupted "by groans and other wilful noises." When he told Maclean that the road to success was through "interesting the understanding of the students by rousing a manly interest of thought," he sealed his fate and was forced to resign.[4]

The bleak conditions Professor Topping described were not unique to Princeton. President Henry Shepherd of the College of Charleston testified in 1892:

> During my own student life at the University of Virginia I cannot recall, in my course of instruction in Latin, a single shadowy reminiscence of aesthetic hint, critical suggestion, culture flavor, or stylistics inspiration. It was a mournful and plaintive round of local relations of prepositions, . . . the distinction between *sic* and *ita, ergo* and *igitur.* . . . Nothing, save my early home environment and my own instinct, preserved me from chaos and disintegration. I survived the ordeal of my university training by a species of literary transcendentalism.[5]

That students were expected to adhere closely to the canon mandated in their prescribed courses and not lose themselves in independent reading was made manifest by library practices. At Princeton in 1868 the library was open to students one hour a week, twice as long as its neighboring college in nearby New Brunswick where the Rutgers library did its business every Saturday morning from eight-thirty to nine. Such restrictive policies

persisted throughout much of the nineteenth century and were
not confined to students. A commonly told anecdote portrayed
President Eliot conversing with his librarian Justin Winsor in
Harvard Yard around 1880. How, Eliot asked, was everything pro-
gressing in the library? "Excellently, excellently," Winsor replied.
"All the books are on the shelf except one that [Professor] Agassiz
has, and I'm going after it now."[6]

The dissemination of knowledge and the inculcation of aesthetic appreciation, then, took a distinctly inferior place to the
much more crucial task of instilling what Maclean referred to as
"mental discipline." The subject of literature, as we know it, was
really not a fixture of American universities until little more than
one hundred years ago, and came into being as a result of a long
acrimonious struggle during which the protectors of the status
quo spoke with religious fervor in defense of a canon they insisted
had been in place through the ages; a canon without which higher
education—and much else—was doomed. In reality, as we have
seen, the classical canon in American colleges was a much
amended reproduction of a medieval curriculum which itself had
already been seriously revised first during the Renaissance and
then during its English adaptation at Oxford and Cambridge. It
was this later version which the Americans inherited and altered to
fit their own needs. The only truly permanent element in the
classical American canon was the belief in its timelessness.

But that belief and the devotion it inspired made change very
difficult for much of the nineteenth century. The situation of
post-classical literature was particularly dismal. "We have known
young men graduate with considerable honor," a Princeton undergraduate wrote in 1844, "who knew absolutely nothing of history and of Shakespeare and Milton, and Spenser and Dryden, of
Swift, Addison and Johnson." Thomas Lounsbury, who graduated from Yale in 1859, told Professor Brander Matthews that during his studies there "he never heard the name of any author of
our language." In the Harvard catalogue for 1868–69, a single

elective entitled "English" was offered, and it *ended* with Anglo-Saxon and Chaucer. As late as 1894 Professor Katherine Lee Bates of the Wellesley College Department of English Literature still referred to the teaching of her subject, which encompassed the language of her nation and her culture, as "the modern experiment" and worried publicly whether studying it would promote "the disciplined working power of the brain?"[7]

Although Shakespeare was the most popular and ubiquitous playwright in nineteenth-century America and was honored everywhere by a wide spectrum of the population, establishing him in the college canon was no easy matter. Indeed, in 1865 Professor Francis Child, who was to spend most of his career at Harvard teaching English literature, still felt compelled to ask: "But *can* the study of English, the study of Chaucer, Shakespeare, & Milton, say, be made a serious discipline, like the study of Plautus, Lucretius, & Horace?" "I never open my Shakespeare," James Russell Lowell complained in 1887, "but I find myself wishing that there might be professorships established for the expounding of his works." That the mood was changing was evident from Lowell's comment that "there is as much intellectual training to be got from the study of [Shakespeare's] works as from those of any, I had almost said all, of the great writers of antiquity."[8]

President Eliot of Harvard was even more aggressive. He insisted that "the first subject" which deserved to now be included in what he termed "the circle of the arts called liberal," was the English language and its literature. "Greek literature," he asserted, "compares with English as Homer compares with Shakspere, that is, as infantile with adult civilization." "With all this wonderful treasure within reach of our youth," he asked a Johns Hopkins University audience in 1884, "has English literature the foremost place in the programs of schools? By no means; at best only a subordinate place, and in many schools no place at all. Does English take equal rank with Greek or Latin in our colleges? By no means." Here, merely a hundred years ago, we have the spectacle of one of the nation's leading educators imploring his colleagues to include the literature of the English language in the curriculum and the canon.[9]

Although the substance of the classical canon may have faded at the turn of the century, some of its assumptions and methods proved more lasting. Francis March, who became the country's first Professor of English Language in 1857 at Lafayette College, described his "experiment of teaching English like Latin or Greek—hearing a short Grammar lesson, the rest of the hour reading Milton as if it were Homer, calling for the meaning of words, their etymology . . . the relations of words, parsing . . . the connection of clauses." March would have his students conduct "an etymological examination" of a passage from Shakespeare "to ascertain what percentages of his words are derived from Anglo-Saxon, what from Latin, Greek, and other languages," and then prepare statistical tables comparing Shakespeare's use of these words with those of other authors. Fred Lewis Pattee recalled that no class at Dartmouth when he was a student there in the mid-1880s "suggested even remotely that literature is a present-day matter. English literature meant Anglo-Saxon taught as Greek and Latin were taught, Shakespeare, and major English writers taught as something remote and esoteric like Homer or Vergil." The novelist Frank Norris complained that when he studied English literature at Berkeley in the 1890s he was taught to count and tabulate metaphors and similies in a passage and compare the results, discovering that "De Quincey excelled in those metaphors and similies relating to rapidity of movement," and learning in the process more about how to classify than how to write. President Shepherd of the College of Charleston lamented that the same "philological minutiae, phonetic analysis, dialectic investigation" that had plagued his Latin classes were now responsible for "the subordination and repression of the literary sense" in English courses.[10]

The repression, however, does not seem to have penetrated as deeply as it had in the classical curriculum and, unlike poor Professor Evert Topping earlier in the century, no one seems to have

been fired for teaching literature rather than grammar. There were
an increasing number of voices like that of Professor Martin Sampson of Indiana University who described his department's orientation in 1894 as "the study of *literature,* . . . not of grammar,
not of etymology, not of anything except the works themselves,
. . . viewed as art, as transcripts of humanity." Professor Albert
Tolman testified that at the University of Chicago, where English
was the largest department in the university, no longer were "the
stones of learning . . . doled out to students hungry for the bread
of literature." Literary masterpieces were studied "primarily as
works of literary art," not as starting points for "laborious investi-
gations into antiquities, history, geography, etymology, phonetics,
the history of the English language, and general linguistics." *Dial*
magazine, which commissioned and published reports from
twenty college English departments throughout the country at
the close of the nineteenth century, concluded: "'Mere literature'
seems to have its full share of attention and teaching strength; it
appears to be cordially recognized as a true university subject."[11]

The question by then was not whether literature could be
taught as literature rather than as a linguistic vehicle for instilling
mental discipline; it could and increasingly it was. The question
was—and remains—the one Francis March posed to his colleagues
in 1892: "What books, what works shall we choose for study in
schools and colleges?" March's own answer—"Those which contain weighty truths, . . . expressed in musical simplicity, or with
rhythmic distinction"—was not sufficiently explicit to avert the
debate that began as soon as literature in English became a legitimate academic subject.[12]

To comprehend the nature of this debate it is important to
grasp two truths. The first is that as Shakespeare and company
were accepted into the canon they were sacralized, transformed
into "classics," and they began to assume as lofty and unassailable
a position as the Greeks and Romans had enjoyed.[13] Thus while
the contents of the canon may have changed, the *character* of the
canon did not: it remained, theoretically at least, an exclusive

neighborhood open only to a relatively small group of sanctioned works. The second truth derives from the first: for a considerable time in American education, literature in English meant literature exclusively *from* England. Even as the canon became flexible enough to accommodate such postclassical writers as Shakespeare, Spenser, Bacon, Milton, Dryden, Wordsworth, and Tennyson, it remained only partially and grudgingly open to literature in English from the United States and then on the condition that it be classified as part of literature from Britain.

In *A Manual of American Literature* (1873), one of the earliest college textbooks devoted to American writing, John Seely Hart defined his subject as "that part of English literature which has been produced upon American soil." "Properly speaking," a reviewer wrote in the mid-1890s, "there is no such thing [as American literature] unless the pictorial scratchings of aborigines on stones and birch bark are to be classed as literary productions." In *An Introduction to American Literature* (1898) Henry Pancoast insisted that American literature "means simply the American branch of English literature set by colonization in fresh earth; . . . Our true place in literary history is as one of the literatures of this greater England." When Fred Lewis Pattee asked in the *Dial* in 1896, "Is There an American Literature?" and answered by asserting that "Men like Cooper and Whitman and Mark Twain would have been impossible on any other soil. . . . [The United States] has a distinct literature, no matter what may be the language in which it is written," he was censured in a *New York Times* editorial, treated to what he called "instant and devastating criticism," and "deluged" with sarcastic letters. "Most of the criticisms," he recalled many years later, "were tinged with rancor, as if I had profaned sacred ground."14

In the introduction to his 1922 collection of essays, *Civilization in the United States,* Harold E. Stearns declared: "whatever else American civilization is, it is not Anglo-Saxon," and warned that "we shall never achieve any genuine nationalistic self-consciousness as long as we allow certain financial and social minorities to persuade us that we are still an English Colony. Until we begin seriously to appraise and warmly to cherish the heterogeneous elements which make up our life, and to see the common element running through all of them, we shall make not even a step towards true unity." Stearn's advice was largely lost on the academic world in general and particularly on the departments of English which, in Howard Mumford Jones's words, took the view that "American literary history is an appendix to British literary history, a tail on the British lion." "I have done my best to keep courses in American literature from flourishing too widely," Lane Cooper, a professor of English at Cornell, wrote a colleague. He argued that courses in American literature "have done harm by diverting . . . attention from better literatures. I suppose there are advocates for the teaching of Australian literature in Australia, Bolivian literature in Bolivia, and so on. . . . There was no teaching of American literature as such in my day at Rutgers."[15]

In 1922 Arthur Hobson Quinn studied seventeen leading universities and found that only three (Columbia, Michigan, and Pennsylvania) offered a graduate course in American literature every year while three (Brown, Johns Hopkins, and Princeton) taught no American literature at the graduate level at all. Quinn was concerned that while he found "no lack of interest on the part of graduate students in the subject," they had little opportunity to nurture and develop that interest. Robert E. Spiller, one of Quinn's graduate students at the University of Pennsylvania, recalled that when he was a student in the teens and twenties "an American specialization was hardly respectable; in fact, it was close to professional suicide." "American scholarship and education in the field of the national letters have till recently merited shame rather than pride," Norman Foerster observed in 1928. "In general it has been a subject attractive to facile journalists and ignorant dilettanti, and repellent to sound but timorous scholars." During these years American universities offered as much graduate work in Chaucer as in all of American literature. F. O. Matthiessen, who graduated from Yale in 1923 with a B.A. in literature, did not begin to read American authors until a stay in Europe after graduation. He read *Leaves of Grass* in England and *Walden* during a trip up the Rhine. He entered Harvard in 1925 determined to write a doctoral dissertation on Walt Whitman but was persuaded by his professors to write on something more significant: Elizabethan translation.[16]

This situation, of course, profoundly affected undergraduate teaching since there were so few professors versed in American literature. In 1928 Ferner Nuhn found that in American colleges and universities Scandinavian literature was taught as often as American literature, Italian literature twice as often, Spanish and German literature three times as often, French literature four times as often, Latin and Greek literature five times as often, and English literature ten times as often. More undergraduate courses were devoted to two English poets, Chaucer and Milton, than were offered in all of American literature. Thirteen years later, Floyd Stovall surveyed seventy English departments and found that American literature constituted no more than 20 percent of the offerings.[17]

Howard Mumford Jones read a despairing paper before the 1935 Modern Language Association meeting in which he announced to his colleagues that his examination of the Association's scholarly journal from its inception in 1884 revealed that of the 1,405 articles published in fifty years, "only forty-five have had anything to do with American letters, and only twenty-nine of the forty-five have dealt directly with American literature as such." This supported his survey of twenty-five leading colleges and universities in which "there has been only the most elementary treatment of the subject." In this country, he concluded, "not only the undergraduates, but our doctors of philosophy are primarily specialists in the literature of a foreign land. . . . We require them to know Chaucer and Shakespeare, Milton and Swift, Wordsworth and Browning, but when it is a question of familiarizing them with the line of geniuses which begins with Franklin and extends to Whitman and beyond, we display only a tepid interest."

In that same year, George Santayana made a similar point in his novel *The Last Puritan*. When Oliver Alden, a bright high school student, admits that he has never read Walt Whitman and did not even realize Whitman was American, his father explains, "Oliver has been brought up on the classics, and Walt Whitman isn't yet counted among them, at least not in our family." Precisely the same thing could have been said of such now canonized writers as Melville, Twain, Emerson, Thoreau, Henry James, and Emily Dickinson.[18]

"Where," Leonard Koester asked in 1940 "is the American Department" in which American culture can be organized and presented? It did not exist because "our colleges and universities neglect our own culture . . . shamefully." It was difficult to tell from an American university catalogue that we were no longer an English colony. Literature departments offered courses in Old English, Middle English, Shakespeare, the English Romanticists, the English Novel. "At the end of the list there is a course in American literature, with perhaps one in American culture." The only way to break the cycle was to create an American Department. Once it exists, Koester insisted, "students will awaken to the existence of an American culture. Men of ability will specialize in phases of it, just as they specialize in Shakespeare now." Ferner Nuhn's survey twelve years earlier had led him to the same conclusion: only the establishment of departments of American literature could create "something like a decent academic respect for the natural culture of the Republic." It seemed little enough to ask, he contended, "that the national literature be granted a status equal to that now generally accorded such subjects as journalism, the Spanish language and literature, band instruments, horticulture, animal husbandry, and military science and tactics."[19]

One inescapable conclusion that emerges from all of this is that just as little more than one hundred years ago American college students studied a canon in which English literature had a minor role, so as recently as fifty years ago they studied a canon in which the literature of their own culture played a negligible part.

World War II was to change this, though the change was hardly instantaneous. As late as 1948 a committee appointed by the National Council of Teachers of English concluded that "American literature, in spite of its recent expansion, still constitutes only a small part of all the work covered by college English teachers." The growth of courses in American literature has "hardly kept pace with the additions that have been made in the field of English literature." One institution gave students the opportunity to study Anglo-Saxon religious poetry but not American literature while others devoted as much course time to such subjects as Old Irish or the Celtic influences on English literature as to American literature. Less than 5 percent of all American universities and colleges required a course in American literature for the bachelor's degree and less than a quarter required American literature courses for those majoring in English. At Yale University in 1952 William Goetzmann had to transfer to American Studies in order to write his doctoral dissertation on Thomas Wolfe because the English Department did not consider Wolfe an author appropriate for literary study. It was in 1952 as well that Robert Hutchins wrote in the introduction to his fifty-four volume *Great Books of the Western World:* "I omitted Emerson, Whitman, Thoreau, and Mark Twain . . . [because] only the writers that seemed indispensable could be included." Nevertheless, though no miraculous transformations occurred, the sense of nationalism and of national concern, fostered by both the Second World War and its Cold War aftermath, fortified the position of those who had been working to legitimize the study of American culture in the academy.[20]

During the war, Alfred Kazin observed that the "enormous body of writing devoted to the American scene" and the remarkable "experience in national self-discovery" which had characterized the Depression decade was being intensified by "the sudden emergence of America as the repository of Western culture in a world overrun by Fascism." Kazin left it to the Axis ministers of culture "to impose an external unity upon culture; it is only those who have . . . no belief in culture who resent differences

among men and the explorations of the human imagination."
Kazin's splendid study of modern American literature, *On Native
Grounds* (1942), in which these words appeared, was one such
exploration and Kazin called for more. Robert Spiller utilized the
crisis of war to remind his colleagues how little they were contributing to their students' knowledge of American culture: "We
are willing to shout our approval of American civilization and culture, but when we sit down to serious study, we invariably turn to
the cultures of other times and other peoples." It was time "to
study ourselves confidently and critically in order to gain so thorough a knowledge of our past and present that it may be a flexible
instrument for the shaping of our future." The study of American
culture, he declared, "must become the center and the guiding
principle of our entire scheme of liberal education from the earliest grades to the most abstruse levels of graduate research."[21]

These sentiments were reaffirmed by President Franklin Roosevelt who told the Association of American Colleges that he was
anxious that the war not impair or threaten the colleges "which
have contributed so largely to the development of American culture" and which were necessary to help "guarantee the preservation of those aspects of American life for which the war is fought."
His administration's Serviceman's Readjustment Aid Act of 1944
(the "G.I. Bill") which helped millions of veterans begin or
resume their studies, as well as such postwar government programs as building American libraries featuring American literature
and culture, promoting American Studies programs, and sponsor-
ing the work of American artists and musicians in performances
and exhibitions throughout Europe, Asia, and Africa, helped to
validate and encourage the study of things American.[22]

Robert Spiller recalled that when he joined the English Department at the University of Pennsylvania toward the close of the war
and taught its first graduate course in twentieth-century American literature, "I soon found that I had more dissertations to
supervise than I could possibly handle." This mirrored the
national situation. From 1948 to 1955 roughly 100 dissertations in

American literature were produced each year, increasing to an average of 135 from 1955 to 1961. More dissertations were written on American literary topics in this thirteen-year period than had been written from the first American literature dissertation in 1891 until 1948. While there was still much room for improvement, marked progress had been made on the undergraduate level as well. Of the 711 universities and colleges listed in the *Educational Directory* for 1946–47, only nine or ten offered no courses in American literature.[23]

There was also a great expansion of interdisciplinary programs in American Civilization and American Studies in which literature played a major role. Before the war there had been a handful of these programs at such schools as Amherst, Chicago, George Washington, Harvard, Pennsylvania, Smith, Western Reserve, Wisconsin, and Yale. During and immediately after the war the number of such programs proliferated with more than a dozen being introduced in the academic year 1945–46 alone. By 1948 more than sixty institutions offered the B.A. degree and approximately fifteen offered graduate degrees in American Civilization or American Studies. By 1973, of the 1700 four-year academic institutions in the country, one in seven offered an American Studies degree. The growth and expansion of these programs was aided immeasurably by grants from such sources as the Carnegie Corporation and the Rockefeller Foundation. By 1958, 20 percent of American Studies programs had received funding from outside their own institutions.[24]

Obviously, there were more than a few who agreed with Tremaine McDowell of the University of Minnesota that American Studies were important to "the creation of world order." An enlightened American nationality, he argued, was essential to "an effective league of mankind. Self-knowledge is therefore a prerequisite to citizenship both in the United States and in a world community." The political thrust in these remarks became far more overt in the bequest of more than a million dollars the Coe Foundation made to Stanford University to establish and maintain a program of American Studies "designed to combat in a positive and affirmative way the threat of communism, socialism, totalitarianism, collectivism, and other ideologies opposed to our American System of Free Enterprise."[25]*

The conviction that the study of American literature had a role to play in the determination of international issues was reinforced by the worldwide postwar fascination with American culture. When he arrived in Oslo as Fulbright professor in January, 1950, Robert Spiller found that Arthur Miller's *Death of a Salesman* was playing in the Norwegian National Theater, a prominent bookstore featured a window display of Norman Mailer's *The Naked and the Dead,* the university's American Institute had a fine collection of modern American literature, and the leading Norwegian publisher, Gyldendahl, was devoting half of its "Golden Series" of translations of contemporary authors to American works. This scenario was repeated in nation after nation. Spiller wondered: "Was it the emerging political world power of the United States or was it appreciation of literary excellence that made for this popularity with both the public and the scholar?"[26] In fact, those two elements were probably less separable than Spiller imagined.

This was not the first time that a foreign war had profoundly affected the American college curriculum, as we saw earlier. Ironically, the same mechanism that had helped ensconce Western Civ in the curriculum was to help dislodge it several decades later. World War II, and its aftermath, simultaneously undermined the hegemony of Western Civ on American campuses and helped to promote the study of American literature and culture.

---

*In his recollections, *Exemplary Elders,* David Levin has described how the terms of this bequest prevented Irving Howe, who edited the socialist journal *Dissent,* from becoming Stanford's first William Robertson Coe Chair in American literature and American studies in the early 1960s. The English department protested but refused to request that the university return the Coe money if Howe was ruled ineligible because of his political beliefs. Howe joined the department without the chair.

The history of American literature on campus makes clear once again the evolving openness of the university curriculum as it responded to a changing society and world. When we learn how recently contested such "classics" as *Moby Dick, Leaves of Grass,* and Emily Dickinson's poetry were, we should at the very least gain enough perspective to comprehend more clearly and respond more thoughtfully and sensitively to the similar struggles of our own day.

Canons and Culture

The manner in which Western Civ declined and American literature and American Studies emerged in the canon and the curriculum teaches us once again that canons do not reside in some protected galaxy of universal truths beyond the reach of merely temporal events. This is not to say that a canon is defenseless; a canon does possess some weapons which help shield it against the effects of the events transpiring around it. Not permitting someone like F. O. Matthiessen to write on Walt Whitman or trying to prevent William Goetzmann from focusing his dissertation on Thomas Wolfe is only one of the ways the canon has been protected within the academy. More commonly and more subtly the canon itself has functioned to help make students or scholars not *want* to write about a certain author or type of work.

As Jane Tompkins has put it: "An admission of ignorance about [James Fenimore] Cooper, among English department members, is less a shameful confession than a subtle boast," because of what were deemed to be Cooper's egregious failings, not the least of which was his melodramatic "sensationalism." Though her field of specialization was nineteenth-century American literature and

Cooper was one of the most widely read of that century's writers, Tompkins completed her Ph.D. and several years of college teaching without having read any of Cooper's novels since she was nine. When a course she was teaching finally compelled her to read *The Last of the Mohicans,* she was amazed by Cooper's complexity. "I began to see him as a profound thinker, . . . I decided that Cooper was an author whom I had been prevented from reading by prejudices formed during my education." She not only had been taught to ignore Cooper, her training had not prepared her to approach him: "His work seemed powerful and moving in the teeth of a hundred well-known faults, but I could not explain its power or its intricacy in any literary vocabulary that was available to me."[1]

Tompkins's experiences with Cooper were true of many other authors now deemed standard, such as Herman Melville, whose elevation into the canon was torturously slow and often accompanied by bitter debate and intense resistance. Despite the resistance, the canon remained in a constant state of flux. The ways in which the canon constantly changed are illustrated by Paul Lauter in his comparison of two volumes edited by Norman Foerster. The first, published in 1916, presented the work of nine American writers who had become "by general consent, the American prose classics." The second, published in 1963, featured eight writers who "in the consensus of our time . . . constitute our 'American Classics.'" Only three writers—Poe, Emerson, and Hawthorne—made both lists. Foerster's dramatic shifts concerning who deserved to be at the canonical apex were not atypical. As the twentieth century progressed, writers like Washington Irving, William Cullen Bryant, Harriet Beecher Stowe, James Russell Lowell, Henry Wadsworth Longfellow, John Greenleaf Whittier, Edith Wharton, and William Dean Howells fell from favor, while such authors as Herman Melville, Walt Whitman, Mark Twain, Henry James, Henry David Thoreau, and Emily Dickinson rose in esteem.[2]

But even for an author like Nathanial Hawthorne, whose entry into the canon was relatively easy and who has been in it for a very long time, the process is intensely complex. While Hawthorne's reputation has been durable, the *bases* for his position as a "classic" writer have by no means remained stable. Critics in the nineteenth century often appreciated different works of Hawthorne than critics a hundred years later. More crucially, even when critics esteemed the same works, they commonly did so for different reasons. That is, though Hawthorne remained canonized throughout, the reasons for his canonization—the meaning of his writings and the cultural values he ostensibly represented—varied markedly because the culture, the values, the very assumptions of his readers changed through the generations, which in turn altered the ways in which they read Hawthorne and the meanings they found in him. As Jane Tompkins has put it: "*The Scarlet Letter* is a great novel in 1850, in 1876, in 1904, in 1942, and in 1966, but each time it is great for different reasons. . . . The novel Hawthorne produced in 1850 had a specificity and a force within its own context. . . . But as the context changed, so did the work embedded in it." Thus what appears on the surface to be stability is in fact something more intricate and more revealing. The canon changes constantly because historical circumstances and stimuli change and people therefore approach it in myriad ways, bringing different perspectives and needs to it, reading it in ways distinctive to the times in which they live, and emerging with different satisfactions and revelations.[3]

The recurrent transformations of the canon can also be seen, as a number of scholars have demonstrated, by examining the anthologies used widely in American literature courses. These volumes have by no means posited a stable canon of writers whose composition is altered only slowly and deliberately. Quite the contrary.

In his 1873 text, John Seely Hart featured discussions of and examples from literally hundreds of male and female writers including not only novelists and poets but scientists, theologians, historians, and politicians. Hart also found room for a number of popular songs and poems such as *The Old Oaken Bucket:*

> *How dear to this heart are the scenes of my childhood,*
>   *When fond recollection presents them to view;*
> *The orchard, the meadow, the deep tangled wild wood,*
>   *And every loved spot which my infancy knew . . .*

The early twentieth-century anthologies tended to be similarly inclusive. The pioneer American literary scholar Fred Pattee incorporated well over a hundred writers in his *Century Readings for a Course in American Literature* (revised edition, 1922) which he defined as "an interpretation of the American spirit by those who have been our spiritual leaders and our Voices." These "voices," though they remained exclusively White, did include many women, leading politicians and ministers, a variety of humorists, even a few of "the chief American historians," as well as songs and ballads.[4]

By the Great Depression a number of anthologies expanded even further to embrace a wide variety of folklore including African American and Native American lyrics, poems, and tales. In his popular *American Poetry from the Beginning to Whitman* (1931), Louis Untermeyer observed that long before Columbus "discovered" America, poetry existed here in the form of "the lyrics as well as the song-and-dance rituals of the Indians" who were "the earliest of our poets." Similarly, he disputed the assertion that John Smith was "our first American author," noting that "the Spanish Colonial poetry of the Southwest" antedated "the derivative English poetry of the East." Thus, in addition to a wide array of poets from Anne Bradstreet to Whitman, he organized materials under such rubrics as "American Indian Poetry," "Spanish-Colonial Verse," "Early American Ballads," "Negro Spirituals," "Negro Social, 'Blues' and Work-Songs," "Cowboy Songs and Hobo Harmonies," "Backwoods Ballads," and "City Gutturals." In his widely used *Modern American Poetry* (1930, 1936),

Untermeyer included works by the African American poets Paul Laurence Dunbar, James Weldon Johnson, Claude McKay, Countee Cullen, Jean Toomer, and Langston Hughes.[5]

In the decades following World War II, as American literature was becoming more firmly lodged in American colleges, the range of literature anthologies narrowed considerably. Thus Professor Perry Miller of Harvard announced in 1962 that now that American literature was established "as a reputable and incontestable subdivision of the English department," it was no longer necessary to be so broad and inclusive in representing it. "As the age of discovery and of elementary mapping closes," he announced, "the era of evaluation opens. . . . It is incumbent upon us to make clear which are the few peaks and which the many low-lying hills. We must, if we can, suppress an undiscriminating pedantry by distinguishing just wherein the great are truly great. We must set apart those who belong to world literature rather than merely to local (or, to what is worse, regional) patriotism." Thus he and his co-editors found room for only twenty-eight "superior" writers in the 2,056 pages of *Major Writers of America*. Three years earlier, Leon Edel and three colleagues had been even more selective in devoting the 1,846 pages of their *Masters of American Literature* to "eighteen master authors of our native tradition." The numbers were further reduced in William Gibson and George Arms, *Twelve American Writers* (1962), and Norman Foerster and Robert Falk, *Eight American Writers* (1963).[6]

These increasingly exclusive volumes completely ignored the oral and folk literature that had been included in earlier anthologies, no longer reprinted excerpts from influential popular volumes or widely performed ballads and poems, had no space for even such major Black writers as W. E. B. Du Bois, Frederick Douglass, Langston Hughes, Zora Neale Hurston, or Richard Wright, bypassed the entire southwestern United States as well as Native American and immigrant writers of any kind, and provided at best only token space for women writers. This is the exceedingly cramped canon that has been augmented and deepened in the past few decades in such volumes as *The Heath Anthology of American Literature* and *The Harper American Literature* which make it unmistakably clear how culturally diverse and remarkably dynamic American literature has been and continues to be. In these comprehensive volumes students can experience for themselves the "wide range of distinctive voices" that attest to what Donald McQuade, the general editor of the Harper anthology, calls the "inexhaustible richness" of American literature.[7]

The American literary canon, then, has expanded and contracted throughout this century and its volatility was by no means introduced in our time. As Harold Kolb recently put it: "If a canon is a national repository, it is one in which our citizens are constantly making deposits and withdrawals." And, I would add, these deposits and withdrawals are not made in some abstract context of eternal standards and values but in the context of the surrounding culture, its values and needs.[8]

A somewhat different dynamic has informed the historical canon which unlike the literary canon is composed not of authors and texts but of events and contexts. In many of its characteristics the historical canon is more elusive and less visible than its counterpart in literature. When I did my graduate work at Columbia University in the 1950s, our comprehensive written exams consistently contained a question whose form never varied: "Discuss the changing interpretations of" which was followed by a list of such basic events as American Puritanism, the American Revolution, the creation of the U. S. Constitution, the causes of the Civil War, and so on. We were taught to be comfortable with the fact that our understanding of these standard historical occurrences tends to vary from generation to generation since we inevitably view the past through the flawed spectacles of the present.

The acceptance of change, then, has been built into the historical canon to such an extent that it often appears that there *is* no canon. But the moment change goes beyond merely the meanings of well-agreed-upon standard events and begins to revolve around the question of *which* events and *which* people should constitute the focus of historical study in the first place, then the existence of a canon becomes manifest and the same fierce resistance to its alteration is often evident.

This was and is clear in the struggles that have accompanied the expansion of the historical discourse in the twentieth century into such once relatively uncharted areas as the history of African Americans, women, workers, immigrant communities, gays and lesbians, and such neglected subjects as folklore and popular culture. It was just as this expansion was taking place that we began to hear the familiar cries of political correctness, pleas for synthesis, and accusations that historians were abandoning their former communication with the general public.

The contemporary literary and historical canons, like those that preceded them, have been shaped by deep social and cultural forces. But while these forces may produce change, they don't, as we've already seen, produce easy or immediate acceptance of change. Curricular revisions, due to the cultural dissonance they often produce, are no simpler today than they were a century ago.

How do people educated in one course of thought modify a curriculum to accommodate and comprehend other lines of thought and experience? *Not easily!* People educated to believe that only certain forms of culture—classical music, for example—are worthy of study in a university are upset to see the introduction of courses dealing with jazz, blues, or country music. People educated to believe that history means narrative accounts of the powerful and influential leaders of society are disconcerted to see the emergence of a scholarship based upon a more inclusive historical approach. People educated to believe that one part of the world, Western Europe, contributed everything culturally worthwhile in American society are confused and even angered by the rise of a scholarship based upon the idea that other peoples may well have influenced seriously the formation of American culture, character, and society and are therefore worthy of study and understanding.

This discomfort shouldn't surprise us any more than the fact that in the past those educated to believe that the Earth was the center of the universe and that humankind was the essential center of the Earth were distressed by the introduction into the curriculum of sciences which weren't quite so sure of either proposition. There was a good deal of turmoil when those sciences—Darwinian biology, for example—were introduced into the curriculum, just as there is turmoil in our own day when new approaches to history and literature are introduced. The fact is, of course, that teaching subjects in schools and colleges gives them cultural legitimacy. And what we're witnessing in our society at present is a struggle over legitimacy, which explains why the current confrontation over the curriculum and the canon is so intense and so public.

The debate over the canon has been dominated by the fear that the canon is finite; add something and something else must be deleted. The fact is that if there ever was a time when universities could teach the entire canon, or even the entire canon in any single subject area, that time has long passed as the proponents of the elective system recognized more than a hundred years ago. George Perkins Marsh in his 1847 Phi Beta Kappa address at Harvard declared that knowledge had so expanded that "none can hope to possess it in its full extent. . . . He therefore who aspires to be initiated into the mysteries of science must elect his faculty, and choose ignorance of some things well worthy to be understood, to the end that he may the more perfectly know and appropriate those truths for the investigation of which he has a special vocation." Similarly, Charles Eliot in his 1885 debate with President McCosh of Princeton, described in Chapter 2, argued that in the modern world it was impossible "for one mind to compass more than an insignificant fraction of the great sum of acquired knowledge," and concluded that therefore universities had to encourage "diversity" in their canons and curricula.[9]

Thus canonical works can retain their importance even if not all of them are taught at any given point to any given individual, which in fact has become the standard operating procedure: students and faculty can only taste—not to mention digest—portions of the canon, and indeed there are entire canons that they never begin to approach. Stephen Graubard, who in the 1950s taught one of the history courses at Harvard that were instituted in lieu of a general Western Civ course, recalled that "no single course, even then, could possibly accommodate all the classics of the Western tradition." Instead, students were allowed to choose among a number of offerings. In the course on "Freedom and Authority in the Modern World" which Graubard helped to develop, the assigned readings included works by Karl Mannheim, Jacques Maritain, Joseph Schumpeter, Sigmund Freud, and Bertrand de Jouvenal: "The books were undoubtedly 'great,' but over a nine-year period we changed them periodically, not necessarily for greater ones but for others that would more fully serve our pedagogic purposes."[10]

Of course the very expansiveness of the canon is disturbing to those who crave a universal literary or historical canon good always and everywhere, accessible to and accepted by everyone capable of understanding it. The admission that literature, history, *and* canons are more complex and more variable than that entails a loss of control and an acceptance of the truth that the academic world, like the larger universe, is more chaotic, less ordered, less predictable and more affected by such matters as geography, class, race, ethnicity, gender than many of us have been willing to accept. The idea that somehow the canon transcends the real world and exists in some ideal universe where pure values and eternal verities are free to assert themselves retains its appeal but remains as chimerical as ever. The university, for all its privileges, *is* the real world, and its canons have always reflected the temporal aspects of that larger society of which it was—and is—part.

By now most of us know this intellectually but somehow we continue to pine for that ethereal world emotionally, and we need constant reminders of the ways in which canons really work. Although there is almost never perfect consonance between the canon and the culture, the canonical inevitably is affected by cultural circumstances and transformations as we have seen. The rise of industrial America finally led to the demise of the classical curriculum and the adoption of the elective system; World War I promoted a sense of Western civilization; World War II and the Cold War heightened the sense of Americanness and a concern with things American. The rise of the Third World, the decline of European hegemony, the civil rights and women's movements, and the entry of new ethnic and racial minorities into the academic world as both students and teachers during the past several decades have promoted significant cultural and canonical changes which numerous colleagues have rejected as somehow uniquely political—overly tainted by the secular and the immediate rather than the sacred and the timeless, which is the way they have imagined canons to be.

Alvin Kernan, whose views concerning the "death of literature" I discussed earlier, admits that the canon he is mourning is part of a larger complex of values and institutions that has been altered by modernity. Kernan's concerns go beyond literature: "Not only the arts but all our traditional institutions, the family and the law, religion and the state, have in recent years been coming apart in startling ways. . . . The death throes of the nuclear family, along with the changes in other major social institutions, make the death of romantic literature seem but a trifle here."[11]

One does not have to share Kernan's pessimism to share his understanding that the disquiet about contemporary changes in the canonical is tied to and part of a larger anxiety concerning the directions in which our society seems to be moving. The debate over the canon is now, and has always been, a debate over the culture and over the course that culture should take. This insight may not help us determine which side in the debate to take, but it should enable us to fathom that it is not a debate between History and Expediency, the Sacred and the Profane, Permanence and Instability, the High and the Low, Culture and Vulgarity, the Really Correct and the Merely Politically Correct.

Nor is this debate an aberrant product of a debased society; it is the current chapter of a much older and continuing discussion about values, meanings, perspectives, and ways of comprehending ourselves and those around us. What we inside and outside the academe need to do is worry less about what any specific canon contains and more about the nature of canons themselves: how they are constituted, what they represent, and how and why they change. If we understood the canonical process and dynamic better than we do, if we had a truer comprehension of the canon's relationship to the larger culture, we would more clearly understand the process of change within the university—and within our society as well.

The debate over the nature of the curriculum and the canon was paralleled by a debate that raged throughout the whole of American history over the nature of America itself and of American identity. In an immigrant country how did one become American and what in fact did that term mean in the first place? This debate has been integral to the debates over the curriculum and canon. *Who* we are, *where* our culture derives from, and *what* it is composed of, all help determine our educational needs and goals. Multiculturalism may be a relatively new term, but the debate over multiculturalism is an old one that has occupied us from early in our existence as a people. To fully understand the issues raised in this book thus far, it is necessary to turn to the hotly contested subject of American identity.

The Search for American Identity

I'm an Anglo-Saxon. . . . Th' name iv Dooley has been th'
proudest Anglo-Saxon name in th' county Roscommon f'r
many years. . . . Pether Bowbeen down be th' Frinch church is
formin' th' Circle Francaize Anglo-Saxon club, an' me ol'
frind Dominigo . . . will march at th' head iv th' Dago
Anglo-Saxons whin th' time comes. There arre twinty thou-
san' Rooshian Jews . . . in th' Sivinth Ward; an', ar-rmed
with rag hooks, they'd be a tur-r-ble thing f'r anny inimy iv
th' Anglo-Saxon 'lieance to face. Th' Bohemians an' Pole
Anglo-Saxons may be a little slow in wakin' up to what th'
pa-apers calls our common hurtage, but ye may be sure
they'll be all r-right whin they're called on. . . .

I tell ye, whin . . . th' Sons iv Sweden . . . an' th' Circle Fran-
caize an' th' Pollacky Benivolent Society an' th' Rooshian
Sons of Dinnymite an' th' Benny Brith . . . an' th' Holland
Society an' th' Afro-Americans an' th' other Anglo-Saxons
begin f'r to raise their Anglo-Saxon battle-cry, it'll be all
day with th' eight or nine people in th' wurruld that has th'
misfortune iv not bein' brought up Anglo-Saxons.

Finley P. Dunne, *Mr. Dooley in Peace and in War,* 1898

The United States themselves are essentially the greatest
poem. . . . Here is not merely a nation but a teeming nation
of nations.

Walt Whitman, Preface, *Leaves of Grass,* 1855

From the Melting Pot to the Pluralist Vision

From the beginning of our history, Americans have been alternately (and sometimes simultaneously) fascinated and frightened by a query that was articulated in its classic form by Alexis de Tocqueville in a letter to Ernest de Chabrol in the spring of 1831: "Imagine, my dear friend, if you can, a society formed of all the nations of the world . . . people having different languages, beliefs, opinions: in a word, a society without roots, without memories, without prejudices, without routines, without common ideas, without a national character, yet a hundred times happier than our own." This portrait led Tocqueville to ask the question that has so preoccupied Americans: "What serves as the link among such diverse elements? What makes all of this into one people?"[1]

Almost fifty years before Tocqueville posed his question, another Frenchman, Hector St. John de Crèvecoeur, who was not a visitor like Tocqueville but an immigrant, had described a similarly heterogeneous people, and to his own question, "What, then, is the American, this new man?" he responded: *"He* is an American, who, leaving behind him all his ancient prejudices and manners, receives new ones from the new mode of life he has embraced, the new government he obeys, and the new rank he holds. He becomes an American by being received in the broad lap of our great Alma Mater. Here individuals of all nations are melted into a new race of men, whose labours and posterity will one day cause great changes in the world." Like Frederick Jackson Turner a hundred years later, Crèvecoeur utilized metaphors of nature and the soil. "Men are like plants, the goodness and flavour of the fruit proceeds from the peculiar soil . . . in which they grow." In the free, unspoiled soil of America the immigrant underwent a "resurrection," and became "a new man, who acts upon new principles."[2]

Here were the seeds of the idea of the melting pot, the most popular and long-lived explanation of what transforms a polyglot stream of immigrants into one people. The notion of the melting pot was a revolutionary theory of identity. American identity was not static but progressive and ever-changing depending on what went into the great crucible in which that identity was forged. In 1845 Ralph Waldo Emerson noted in his *Journal* that "man is the most composite of creatures," and used the analogy of the burning of the Temple of Corinth in which silver, gold, and other metals intermixed and created a new, stronger compound called Corinthian brass: "so in this Continent, —asylum of all nations, the energy of Irish, Germans, Swedes, Poles, & Cossacks, & all the European tribes, —of the Africans, & of the Polynesians, will construct a new race, a new religion, a new State, a new literature." Herman Melville was hardly less enthusiastic. "We are not a narrow tribe of men," he insisted in 1849, ". . . whose blood has been debased in the attempt to ennoble it, by maintaining an exclusive succession among ourselves. No: our blood is as the flood of the Amazon, made up of a thousand noble currents all pouring into one. We are not a nation, so much as a world. . . . Our ancestry is lost in the universal paternity. . . . On this Western Hemisphere all tribes and people are forming into one federated whole."[3]

Frederick Jackson Turner embodied the same confidence in the uniqueness of what was transpiring in the United States. In 1893 he insisted, as we have seen, that "in the crucible of the frontier the immigrants were Americanized, liberated, and fused into a mixed race, English in neither nationality nor characteristics. The process has gone on from the early days to our own." The Middle West, he wrote in a later essay, was demonstrating "the possibility of a newer and richer civilization, not by preserving unmodified or isolated the old component elements, but by breaking down the line-fences, by merging the individual life in the common product a new product, which held the promise of world brotherhood."[4]

One hundred and twenty-six years after the French immigrant Crèvecoeur used the term "melting" to describe the process of identity formation in America, an English Jewish immigrant, Israel Zangwill, wrote a play called *The Melting Pot* (1908) which permanently fused that term to the process. The play's hero, David Quixano, a Russian Jewish immigrant composer, speaks of the United States as "God's Crucible, the great Melting-Pot where all the races of Europe are melting and re-forming!" The real American, David tells his uncle, had not yet arrived. "He is only in the Crucible, I tell you—he will be the fusion of all races, perhaps the coming superman." Like Emerson's "smelting pot," Zangwill's melting pot was inclusive. While early in the play David speaks only of Europeans, by the finale he stares at New York's harbor through which the immigrants pour and exclaims: "Ah, what a stirring and seething! Celt and Latin, Slav and Teuton, Greek and Syrian, —black and yellow . . . East and West, and North and South, the palm and the pine, the pole and the equator, the crescent and the cross—how the great Alchemist melts and fuses them with his purging flame! Here shall they all unite to build the Republic of Man and the Kingdom of God. . . . where all races and nations come to labour and look forward!"[5]

Because the potential for a dynamic and continuing new cultural synthesis was always present in the various melting pot theories, they posited a dynamic and ever-changing view of national identity which many Americans found too complex, indefinite, and even threatening. No matter how close these theories might have come to describing reality, significant numbers of Americans regarded them with profound ambivalence.

In 1754, several decades before Crèvecoeur wrote, Benjamin Franklin asked why the United States should "darken its People? Why increase the Sons of Africa, by Planting them in America, where we have so fair an Opportunity, by excluding all Blacks and Tawneys [Asians], of increasing the lovely white and Red?" Although he spoke positively of the "Red" race here, he began his original question by speaking ominously of *"Scouring* our Planet" and "clearing America of Woods" thus "making this Side of our Globe reflect a brighter Light to the Eyes of Inhabitants in Mars or Venus." Indeed, Franklin's definition of "White" was quite narrow. "The Number of purely white People in the World is proportionately very small," he wrote. Most Europeans, "the *Spaniards, Italians, French, Russians,* and *Swedes* are generally what we call a swarthy complexion; as are the *Germans* also, the *Saxons* only excepted." It was these Saxons, along with the English, who comprised "the principal Body of white People on the Face of the Earth," and it was to them that Franklin was convinced America should belong. But he tended to express these thoughts with some diffidence: "Perhaps I am partial to the complexion of my Country, for such Kind of Partiality is natural to Mankind."[6]

Franklin's "partiality" is an indication that it would be a mistake to discuss the melting pot by itself; from the beginning there was another, and often quite contrary, set of ideas concerning how American identity was formed which the sociologists Stewart and Mildred Cole have called "Anglo-conformity." This notion insisted that England *was* the Mother Country whose culture and institutions would prevail. When Abraham Reincke, a Swedish Moravian minister, visited settlements of his countrymen along the Delaware River in New Jersey in 1745, he reported: "I found in this country scarcely one genuine Swede left. . . . The English are evidently swallowing up the people and the Swedish language is so corrupted, that if I did not know the English, it would be impossible to understand the language of my dear Sweden." Similarly, David Ramsay in his *History of South Carolina* (1809) wrote that the sources from which South Carolina's population derived were so various that considerable time would pass before Carolinians possessed "an uniform national character." Still, he had no doubt that this day was inevitably drawing nearer: "The different languages and dialects, introduced by the settlers from different countries, are gradually giving place to the English. So much similarity prevails among the descendants of the early emigrants from the old world, that strangers cannot ascertain the original country of the ancestors of the present race."[7]

While one could assert Anglo-conformity as a *fact*—the natural product of climate, form of government, and language—one could also assert it as a *principle*. Those who did so were not content to depend upon natural processes to ensure that immigrants would become Americans through the inexorable workings of time; they *insisted* that immigrants convert willingly and rapidly. The most familiar early example of this attitude is found in a letter Secretary of State John Quincy Adams wrote in 1818 in response to a query concerning immigration by a German nobleman. If immigrants to the United States could not adjust to "the character, moral, political and physical, of this country," Adams exclaimed, "the Atlantic is always open to them to return to the land of their nativity and their fathers." If they wanted to find happiness in their new land, they had to make up their minds to one thing: "They must cast off the European skin never to resume it. They must look forward to their posterity rather than backward to their ancestors; —they must be sure that whatever their own feelings may be, those of their children will cling to the prejudices of this country."[8]

Thomas Jefferson worried about the effects that the mass of European immigrants would have upon the nature of American government and society. In Jefferson's terms it was imperative that there be a conversion to *American* values, principles, and mores lest the European immigrants "warp or bias" the direction of American society and "render it a heterogeneous, distracted mass." His contemporary Dr. Benjamin Rush spoke of the need to convert immigrants into "republican machines" if we expected them to function properly "in the great machine of the government of the state." It was thinking like this, of course, that was in no small part responsible for the continuous emphasis upon education in American thought and action in order to ensure that the feelings of the immigrants' progeny, in Adams's words, "will cling to the prejudices of this country." If American schools produced "one general, and uniform system of education," Rush argued, it would "render the mass of the people more homogenous, and thereby fit them more easily for uniform and peaceable government."[9]

The insistence on conversion links the ideas of the melting pot and Anglo-conformity and makes complete separation of the two concepts difficult; they were easily and frequently consolidated into one. Lewis Gannett recognized this in 1923 when he asserted that "Anglo-Saxon Americans have small interest in the 'melting-pot' except as a phrase. They do not want to be fused with other races, traditions, and cultures. If they talk of the melting-pot they mean by it a process in which the differences of the immigrant races will be carried away like scum, leaving only pure ore of their own traits."[10] Here, then, was a second and very different melting pot than the one posited by Emerson, Melville, Turner, and Zangwill. In my own experiences in the polyglot schools of New York City in the 1930s and 1940s, the melting pot became the instrument by which Anglo-conformity was achieved. Into the pot went the diverse groups and out came Anglo girls and boys, men and women.

That process was graphically illustrated by the Ford Motor Company. Immigrant workers who wanted to join the profit-sharing plan which Ford inaugurated in January, 1914, were compelled to enroll in the Ford English School from which some 16,000 workers graduated before the school was disbanded in 1921. The purpose of the school according to a company spokesman was "to impress these men that they are, or should be, Americans, and that former racial, national, and linguistic differences are to be forgotten." Commencement exercises were held in a large hall. On the stage in front of a model of an immigrant ship stood a huge pot, seven and a half feet high and fifteen feet in diameter. The graduating members of the class, dressed in clothes representative of the nations from which they had come and carrying the types of luggage they had brought with them when they first arrived in the United States, marched down the gangplank from the ship and disappeared into the pot. Six of their teachers then stirred the pot with ten-foot-long ladles. When the pot began to "boil over," the workers emerged, according to an eyewitness, "dressed in their best American clothes and waving American flags."[11]

It was a thoroughly comforting and thoroughly antiseptic notion of acculturation: the outsiders, the strangers, passed through without leaving any trace of themselves, of their cultures, of their identities. They were *processed* as surely and as completely as any other raw materials in the factories of the United States. S. S. Marquis, the head of the Ford Sociological Department, used this very analogy: "This is the human product we seek to turn out, and as we adapt the machinery in the shop to turning out the kind of automobile we have in mind, so we have constructed our educational system with a view to producing the human product in mind." Henry Ford himself once remarked: "I am more a manufacturer of men than of automobiles." *This* was the essence of the modern melting pot as interpreted by Henry Ford in the early twentieth century and, if I recall it correctly, by the New York City schools in the 1930s and 1940s.[12]

In whatever form it took, Anglo-conformity insisted that the immigrants and their progeny had to shed their cultural skins, lose their distinctiveness, and conform to the "standard" American mold which, of course, turned out to be an Anglo American mold. In 1909 the educator Ellwood P. Cubberly expressed his disquiet at the tendency of Southern and Eastern European immigrants to "settle in groups or settlements, and to set up here their national manners, customs, and observances." The task of educators, he asserted, was to "break up these groups or settlements, to assimilate and amalgamate these people as a part of our American race, and to implant in their children, so far as it can be done, the Anglo-Saxon conception of righteousness, law and order, and popular government." In 1918 the superintendent of schools in New York City defined Americanization as entailing not only "an appreciation of the institutions of this country," but also "absolute forgetfulness of all obligations or connections with other countries because of descent or birth." In 1925 Gino Speranza called upon those who like himself were members of Southern or Eastern European ethnic groups to repress their traditional cultures: "the test of service and devotion for the New Stock may be, after all, not how much we give of ourselves, but how much of ourselves we deny. The task and the call for us all—Old Stock and New—as I vision it is to strive to keep America as it was, and, as I pray with all my mind and heart, it may ever be." Americanization entailed, then, not only embracing the new but wiping out all memories and vestiges of the old. As the figure of Uncle Sam on a 1902 poster cautioned immigrants: "Don't say YA—say YES!"[13]

One crucial effect of this doctrine was the difficulty it posed for such racial minorities as Native Americans, Asian Americans, and African Americans who could never conform to the physical dimensions of Anglo-conformity, and for those groups like Catholics, Jews, and Muslims who could conform only by divesting themselves of a set of beliefs at the center of their culture, which, of course, was frequently a problem for racial minorities as well. There were also other important effects. The insistence upon envisioning the United States as a modified English culture blinded generations of Americans to the dynamics and complexities of cultural syncretism whereby American identity and culture were the result not of the *imposition* of English culture on all other groups but of the *interaction* of the various ethnic and racial groups with one another. It especially ruled out any consideration of the influence of African culture in the creation of American culture. Thus in his 1809 history, David Ramsay spoke of the contributions to South Carolina by Scots, Swiss, Irish, Germans, Dutch, and New Englanders without ever alluding to Africans who were then almost half of the population. Crèvecoeur himself shared this myopia when he described "the American, this new man" as "either an European, or the descendant of an European."[14]

It was not until the twentieth century that the stage was set for fundamental departures from prevailing ideas of national identity by the new anthropological definitions of culture which were promulgated around the turn of the century, and which tried to understand diverse cultures from *within* rather than from the imagined heights of European cultural and genetic superiority.

In 1915, Horace Kallen, a Jewish American professor at Columbia University, published two articles in the *Nation* in which he introduced a concept he ultimately called "cultural pluralism" and raised questions which are still very much with us. Kallen pronounced the melting pot a failure. While the immigrant undeniably underwent external changes, he remained an ethnic internally. "Whatever else he changes," Kallen insisted, "he cannot change his grandfather." The immigrant "comes rarely alone; he comes companioned with his fellow nationals; and he comes to no strangers, but to kin and friends who have gone before." In the United States the immigrant "is merely a Dutchman, a Mick, a frog, a wop, a dago, a hunky, or a sheeny and no more; and he encounters these others who are unlike him, dealing with him as a lower and outlandish creature. Then, be he even the rudest and most primeval peasant, heretofore totally unconscious of his nationality, of his categorical difference . . . he must inevitably become conscious of it."

This was an important perception: the process of immigration could strengthen and not merely weaken the ties of ethnicity. In spite of generational changes, acculturation, and intermarriage,

Kallen argued that the ethnic "remains still the Slav, the Jew, the German or the Irish citizen of the American state. . . . Neither he nor his children nor his children's children lose their ethnic individuality." Jews or Poles or Anglo-Saxons, "in order to cease being Jews or Poles or Anglo-Saxons would have to cease to be." Americans were confused about this because "the non-British elements of the population have been practically voiceless." Nevertheless, the truth was that the United States was a cacophony and the question was: "What must, what can, what *shall* this cacophony become—a unison or a harmony?" Kallen did not posit this choice as a metaphor, but as an actual choice: unity or harmony. "To achieve unison . . . would require the complete nationalization of education, the abolition of every form of parochial and private school, the abolition of instruction in other tongues than English, and the concentration of the teaching of history and literature upon the English tradition." He made it clear that this was something akin to European imperialism. It was possible but only at the cost of violating America's own traditions and fundamental principles. The other choice, a "democratic commonwealth" of peoples, a "democracy of nationalities," a "multiplicity in a unity, an orchestration of mankind," was in the American spirit.[15]

The concept of cultural pluralism was an important break with the past tendency of seeing America's constituent groups as undergoing some sort of inexorable processing—either through melting into something else or through conversion to something else. Kallen's writings embodied the notion that continuing cultural and ethnic distinctiveness was not pathological, did not spell the demise of the Republic, but was in fact something to be prized and nurtured.

A year after Kallen, in 1916, Randolph Bourne also spoke of the failure of the melting pot. The advent of war in Europe, Bourne declared, revealed the extent to which immigrants in the United States continued to have deep feelings about their former homelands and made it clear that such immigrant groups as Germans,

Scandinavians, Bohemians, and Poles had not melted but still were in the grip of "vigorous nationalistic and cultural movements." The ubiquitous presence among immigrants of foreign-language schools, newspapers, and organizations was a sign that assimilation "was proceeding on lines very different from those we had marked out for it." The fact that even as immigrant groups became assimilated they tended to retain many of the cultural traditions of their homelands, was "not, however, to admit the failure of Americanization. . . . It is rather to urge us to an investigation of what Americanism may rightly mean." We act, Bourne charged, "as if we wanted Americanization to take place only on our own terms, and not by the consent of the governed." Bourne sympathized with the immigrants' paradoxical situation: on the one hand, they were urged by "hard-hearted old Brahmins" to melt even while those same Brahmins jeered at the pretensions of such newcomers as the Jewish immigrant Mary Antin when she tried to identify with the American past by writing of "our forefathers."

The greatest paradox, Bourne pointed out, was that the would-be processors of immigrants were themselves the products of immigrant cultures. "We are all foreign-born or the descendants of foreign-born, and if distinctions are to be made between us they should rightly be on some other ground than indigenousness." He understood also the importance of the cultural contributions made by the non-English immigrants. "We have needed the new peoples . . . to save us from our own stagnation." He denied the common image which saw the English as assimilated Americans while newer immigrant groups maintained unhealthy and destructive allegiances to their mother lands. "The truth is that no more tenacious cultural allegiance to the mother country has been shown by any alien nation than by the ruling class of Anglo-Saxon descendants in these American states." Indeed, he charged that the cult of "English snobberies, . . . English literary styles, English literary reverences and canons, English ethics, English superiorities" had blinded Americans to the "indigenous genius" of their own traditions and culture which were the product of the variegated groups that composed America. He urged his fellow Americans to understand the "incalculable potentialities" their novel union of diverse peoples gave them and not to settle for the "weary old nationalism, —belligerent, exclusive, inbreeding, the poison of which we are witnessing now in Europe."

Bourne criticized the melting pot paradigm because it cast the American cultural tradition in the past as something to which immigrant groups had to conform. "Our American cultural tradition," he affirmed, "lies in the future. It will be what we all together make out of this incomparable opportunity of attacking the future with a new key." That key was the chance to build a "trans-national" state of many races and peoples, a "world federation in miniature" where for the only time in history the various national groups would both preserve their cultures and identities and join together to create the first truly cosmopolitan international nation which would eschew the "tasteless, colorless fluid of uniformity" and retain the "savor" and strength of ethnic diversity. Immigrants, Bourne insisted repeatedly, were not alien masses "waiting to be melted down into the indistinguishable dough of Anglo-Saxonism. They are rather threads of living and potent cultures," which were endeavoring "to weave themselves into a novel international nation, the first the world has seen." The truest integration, he concluded, would emanate not from "narrow 'Americanism' or forced chauvinism," but from fostering the feeling that "all who are here may have a hand in the destiny of America."[16]

If Kallen and Bourne continued the lamentable practice of basically ignoring non-European racial groups, and especially African Americans, a young Black graduate of Fisk and Harvard universities did not. As early as 1897, W. E. B. Du Bois, with his characteristic originality, explored many of the issues later to interest Kallen and Bourne. He began by asking: "What, after all, am I? Am I an American or am I a Negro? Can I be both? Or is it my duty to cease to be a Negro as soon as possible and be an American? If I strive as a Negro, am I not perpetuating the very cleft that threatens and separates Black and White America?" His answer was unequivocal: the destiny of American Blacks "is *not* absorption by the white Americans. . . . Their destiny is not a servile imitation of Anglo-Saxon culture, but a stalwart originality which shall unswervingly follow Negro ideals." Du Bois insisted that "there is no reason why, in the same country and on the same street, two or three great national ideals might not thrive and develop, that men of different races might not strive together for their race ideals as well, perhaps even better, than in isolation." He called upon "Americans of Negro descent" to maintain their race identity because only as a group could they fulfill themselves as well as continue their essential contributions to the nation in which they lived: "We are that people whose subtle sense of song has given America its only American music, its only American fairy tales, its only touch of pathos and humor amid its mad money-getting plutocracy. As such, it is our duty to conserve our physical powers, our intellectual endowments, our spiritual ideals."[17]

Six years later, in passages that still resonate today, Du Bois wrote of his double-consciousness: "One ever feels his twoness, — an American, a Negro; two souls, two thoughts, two unreconciled strivings; two warring ideals in one dark body." The African American, Du Bois proclaimed, "would not Africanize America, for America has too much to teach the world and Africa. He would not bleach his Negro soul in a flood of white Americanism, for he knows that Negro blood has a message for the world. He simply wishes to make it possible for a man to be both a Negro and an American, without being cursed and spit upon by his fellows, without having the doors of Opportunity closed roughly in his face." Du Bois spoke not of "melting" but of being "a co-worker in the kingdom of culture" where the American Black could utilize "his best powers and his latent genius," which in the past had been "strangely wasted, dispersed, or forgotten," but which the United States desperately needed if it was to fulfill its destiny: "There are to-day no truer exponents of the pure human spirit of the Declaration of Independence than the American Negroes; . . . we black men seem the sole oasis of simple faith and reverence in a dusty desert of dollars and smartness."[18]

At the heart of Kallen's, Bourne's, and Du Bois's arguments was an intriguing perception about the nature and composition of the American people, one which we might imagine historians would have pounced upon and tested. Instead, for more than half a century they almost unanimously ignored it and kept writing as if immigrant groups simply disappeared progressively in the great crucible of American society. There were of course exceptions, such as the sociologist Robert E. Park and a number of his students and colleagues and the historian Marcus Lee Hansen. In 1938 Hansen argued that while the second generation (the children of the immigrant or first generation) "wanted to forget everything"—the language, religion, customs—that had characterized their parents' culture, "wanted to lose as many of the evidences of foreign origin as they could shuffle off," *their* children (the third generation) turned back to the world of their immigrant forebears: "what the son wishes to forget the grandson wishes to remember." Through this mechanism of generational reconstitution, the culture of the immigrants was saved from fading into oblivion and accorded the opportunity for a reinvigorated existence.[19]

For the most part, however, pluralist ideas were overwhelmed by the certainty that ethnic distinctions were in the process of inevitable extinction. In 1964 Milton Gordon concluded that cultural pluralist analyses had not yet "made their way into the thinking of professional intergroup relations workers or the American public—even that segment of the public which is highly literate and keeps abreast of significant current events." As late as 1966 the influential sociologist Talcott Parsons wrote that "emancipation" from such "particularist solidarities" as ethnicity, religion, regionalism, and class was accelerating as society adopted "universalistic norms."[20]

In the past several decades it has become increasingly clear to a growing number of scholars in several disciplines that our society is far more intricate than this, that "universalistic norms" and "particularistic solidarities" might well live side by side, and perhaps had *always* lived side by side throughout American history. Opponents of contemporary scholarship like to portray a wholistic past in which immigrants came to the United States, acculturated promptly and without fuss, and posed no problems for a nation which was inexorably becoming one: one people, one language, one state. In fact, of course, the United States harbored the kernels of division from the beginning and contained a multifarious population distinguished by race, religion, country of origin, philosophy, accent, language, class, and region. Even as the United States was becoming one nation, beckoning to the peoples of the world, expanding its territory, developing its resources, and building its economy, it also remained a divided nation and only 130 years ago barely escaped dissolution in the bloodiest war in our history.

We must not deny this characteristic and historic American flux; we need to recognize it and attempt to understand how it functions, how we have managed to be strong in spite of, indeed, perhaps *because* of the deep divisions and divergences—not all of them ethnic or racial—that define us. Anything less than this sort of honest recognition and comprehension will prevent us from ever answering that query of Tocqueville's: "What serves as the link among such diverse elements? What makes all of this into one people?" The very strength of the United States—its size and diversity—inhibits if it does not make impossible the kind of conventional wholeness and stability that some of us seem to long for and even to invent historically so that the present is made to appear aberrant, and even culpable, for harboring the seeds of separatism and alienation when in fact those seeds have been present and have born fruit throughout our history.

Diversity, pluralism, multiculturalism have been present throughout our history and have acted not merely as the germs of friction and division but as the lines of continuity, the sources for the creation of an indigenous culture, and the roots of a distinctive American identity. We have too often been prevented from understanding this by the diversion of obsolete models and the clamor of archaic debates.

The Troublesome Presence

It is currently popular to write as if those now immigrating to the United States are qualitatively different from any immigrants we have had previously and pose problems of a magnitude we have never before experienced. Thus Arthur Schlesinger, Jr., describes the contemporary United States as "a nation marked by an even stranger mixture of blood than Crèvecoeur had known," laments that "the 'ancient prejudices and manners' disowned by Crèvecoeur have made a surprising comeback," and warns that "the historic idea of a unifying American identity is now in peril." Lawrence Auster assails the belief "that over the next century scores of millions of Hispanics, Asians, Moslems, and Africans can melt into the American character as easily as did the European immigrant groups in the early 20th century," and warns that this new immigration is not just another "wave" of immigrants but an "invasion," which will lead to "the expectation that America must give up its very identity to form a whole new society." Peter Brimelow observes that "there is a sense in which current immigration policy is Adolf Hitler's posthumous revenge on America" because immigration to the United States is "so systematically

different from anything that had gone before as to transform—
and ultimately, perhaps, even to destroy—the one unquestioned
victor of World War II."[1]

Even that venerable elder statesman, George F. Kennan, who in
1947 as "X" alerted us to the Soviet peril, now, in his own name,
warns us against ourselves. There are, he has determined, "far too
many of us" in the United States. Certainly it is important to consider the strains which population growth exerts upon both the
environment and the governmental system. But Mr. Kennan
clearly has more than this on his mind: his worry is not simply that
there are too many of us but more specifically that there are too
many of *some* of us. It is time, he writes, to rethink the assumptions that "there could be no immigrant, of whatever culture or
race or national tradition, who could not be readily absorbed into
our social and political life, could not become infused with understanding for, and confidence in, our political institutions, and
could not, consequently, become a useful bearer of the American
political tradition." We have not understood that "where the dis-
parity between what these people were leaving behind and what
they were coming into was too great, the new arrivals, even in the
process of adjusting to our political tradition, might actually
change it." Conditions "in our major urban ghettos would suggest that there might even be limits to our capacity for assimilation." To underline his point that a culture can be overcome by
what it tries to absorb, he relates a parable:

> The inhabitants of the onetime Italian cities along the
> eastern shore of the Adriatic Sea (the scenes of some of
> Shakespeare's plays) made it a habit, over several centuries, to
> take their menial servants and their ditchdiggers from the
> Slavs of the poorer villages in the adjacent mountains. Today,
> finally, the last of the Italians have left; and the beautiful cities
> in question are inhabited entirely by Slavs, who have little
> relationship to the sort of city and the cultural monuments
> they have inherited. They have simply displaced the original
> inhabitants.

"Surely," he concludes, "there is a lesson in this." And he hammers the lesson home with a second historical analogy featuring the ancient Romans who allowed themselves "to become dependent on the barbarians to fill the ranks of their own armies," which became for them, as it could for us if we continued our dependence on labor imported from the outside, "the beginning of the end." As if to fulfill his own worst fears, Kennan contemplates the possibility of breaking the United States up into twelve "constituent republics" each having control over its own immigration. In such a case, he speculates, "it is not inconceivable that certain of the major southern regions where things have already gone too far would themselves become, in effect, linguistically and culturally, Latin-American countries . . . (which might for them, incidentally, not be the worst of solutions)."[2]

Kennan's vision of the future is not peculiar to him. In 1985 Governor Richard D. Lamm of Colorado called immigration a "time bomb" and spoke of "fears—legitimate fears—that the country is being rejected, or culturally annexed, by its newest immigrants." During the 1994 elections, Linda R. Hayes, the southern California media director for Proposition 187, which denied illegal immigrants in California most government services, warned the nation in a letter to the *New York Times* that the real purpose of those Mexicans who made their way to the United States at considerable risk to themselves and their families was not to find a better life but to return to the very country they had fled, bearing California as their prize: "By flooding the state with 2 million illegal aliens to date, and increasing that figure each of the following 10 years, Mexicans in California would number 15 million to 20 million by 2004. During those 10 years about 5 million to 8 million Californians would have emigrated to other states. If these trends continued, a Mexico-controlled California could vote to establish Spanish as the sole language of California, 10 million more English-speaking Californians could flee, and there could be a state-wide vote to leave the Union and annex California to Mexico."[3]

Of course none of this is new. Every generation has produced its jeremiads about the dangers posed to the nation by the nature and actions of the current crops of immigrants, has fretted about the "barbarians" at the gates, and has predicted, in one way or another, the beginning of the end. Hyperbole and anxiety have been basic components in American discussions of immigration throughout our history.

In 1718 Cotton Mather wondered "what shall be done" with the "great number of people" migrating to Massachusetts "from ye North of Ireland," while one of his fellow Puritans prayed that "their coming so over do not prove fatall in the End." Eighteenth-century political leaders in Pennsylvania worried that the tide of immigration would turn it into a "foreign" colony. Benjamin Franklin complained in 1753 that the Germans, who constituted about one-third of Pennsylvania's population, were so clannish and so insistent upon speaking their native language that it was necessary to have interpreters in order to communicate with them. Unless "the stream of importation" could be diverted to other colonies, "they will soon outnumber us, . . . [and we] will not be able to preserve our language and even our government will become precarious." In that same colony the governor and his secretary complained bitterly about the Scotch Irish: "It looks as if Ireland is to send all its inhabitants hither. . . . It is strange that they thus crowd in where they are not wanted."[4]

Fears of Germans, who often settled together and maintained their distinctive linguistic and cultural traits, continued on well into the nineteenth century and were supplemented by fear of Scandinavians for exactly the same reasons. The arrival of the Protestant Scotch Irish from the north of Ireland had been troubling enough to the Quakers in Pennsylvania and the Puritans in Massachusetts, but the coming of large numbers of Irish Catholic immigrants in the first half of the nineteenth century brought forth frantic anxiety concerning papal dominance and the permanent undermining of Protestant culture in the United States. Widely read fantasies like Samuel Smith's *The Flight of Popery from*

Rome to the West (1836) and Samuel F. B. Morse's *A Foreign Conspiracy Against the Liberties of the United States* (1834) "exposed" the alliance between the Roman church and European monarchs to destroy American republicanism by using Irish and German Catholic immigrants to take control of first the Mississippi Valley and ultimately the entire country. In a warning that anticipated George Kennan's speculation that the American South may ultimately align itself with Latin America, Frederick Marryat predicted in 1839 that "all America west of the Alleghenies will eventually be a Catholic country."[5]

One did not have to believe in conspiracy to complain of the crime, moral intemperance, low standard of living, political corruption, lack of assimilation, and continued allegiance to their former homelands that appeared to characterize immigrants wherever they went. Worst of all, these aliens always seemed just on the verge of taking command: "In fifteen years," John Bell warned in 1855, "the foreign population will exceed the native." George Templeton Strong filled the pages of his diary with complaints about the constant disorder that marred the streets of New York City, much of which he attributed to the "pure Celtic" "rabble" that roamed the city. "An epidemic of crime this winter," he noted in 1857. "'Garotting' stories abound. . . . Most of my friends are investing in revolvers and carry them about at night." In that same year he came across an accident in which two Irish laborers had been killed. He watched and listened with distaste and disbelief as fifteen or twenty Irish women, "kinfolk or friends," bent over the dead bodies "raising a wild, unearthly cry, half shriek and half song, wailing as a score of daylight banshees, clapping their hands and gesticulating passionately. Now and then one of them would throw herself down on one of the corpses, or wipe some trace of defilement from the face of the dead man with her apron, slowly and carefully, and then resume her lament. It was an uncanny sound to hear, quite new to me. . . . Our Celtic fellow citizens are almost as remote from us in temperament and constitution as the Chinese." Not even English immigrants were

immune from condemnation. In 1836 Senator John Davis of Massachusetts rose in the Senate to chastise Great Britain for shipping
"the most idle and vicious" immigrants to America: "Is it morally
right for Great Britain to attempt to throw upon us this oppressive
burden of sustaining her poor? . . . Would it not be wronging our
own virtuous poor to divide their bread with those who have no
just or natural claims upon us? And above all, sir, shall we fold our
arms and see this moral pestilence sent among us to poison the
public mind and do irremediable mischief?"[6]

All of these reproaches were aimed at the very Northern and
Western European peoples who were to become the models of the
Good Immigrant when the turn of the century brought millions
of immigrants from Eastern and Southern Europe and Asia who
now became the focus of the calamitous cries of those who saw
the end of American glory around every corner. The Commission
on Immigration declared in 1911 that the new immigration "is far
less intelligent than the old. . . . Racially they are for the most part
essentially unlike the British, German and other peoples who
came during the period prior to 1880 and generally speaking they
are actuated in coming by different ideals." The large numbers of
Italians streaming into the United States by the 1880s led Josiah
Strong to revive the warnings of immigrant armies dispatched by
the Pope to undermine and conquer Protestant America. The
Jesuits, he cautioned in 1885, "are free to colonize in the great
[American] West, and are there gathering and plotting to Roman-
ize and control our western empire." This had to be resisted at all
costs as did amalgamation with the inferior immigrants of Southern and Eastern Europe. For Strong the American melting pot
had already achieved its end by supplementing the original Anglo-
Saxon colonists with "Celt and Gaul, Welshman and Irishman,
Frisian and Flamand, French Huguenot and German Palatine," a
mixture which would "constitute the new Anglo-Saxon race of
the New World." He predicted that this powerful race "will move
down upon Mexico, down upon Central and South America, out

upon the islands of the sea, over upon Africa and beyond . . . [until] it has Anglo-Saxonized mankind."[7]

There were many who shared Strong's fears of the new immigrants but not his optimism about the Anglo-Saxon future. For them it was already too late: the lion had swallowed the ox, but instead of digesting it, was itself becoming more oxlike. Visiting his native land in 1907 after almost a quarter of a century in Europe, Henry James rode New York City's electric cars and looked into "a row of faces, up and down, terrifying, without exception, to alienism unmistakable, alienism undisguised and unashamed," which made him gasp "with the sense of isolation." He found no escape even in Central Park where the pastoral calm and vernal beauty were disrupted by the "babel" of immigrant tongues, by "the fruit of the foreign trees as shaken down there with a force that smothered everything else." At times James wrote of the new immigrants as if they were creatures from a subhuman world. After walking through the Jewish immigrant Lower East Side, he felt as if he had been "at the bottom of some vast sallow aquarium in which innumerable fish, of over-developed proboscis, were to bump together, for ever, amid heaped spoils of the sea." The dehumanization did not end in these watery depths. He looked out of a window "on a swarming little square in which an ant-like population darted to and fro." The fact that each Jewish immigrant he spied seemed to him a perfect representation of the entire race of Israel reminded him of those "small strange animals . . . snakes or worms, I believe, who, when cut into pieces, wriggle away contentedly and live in the snippet as completely as in the whole." The tenements with their network of fire-escapes resembled a "spaciously organized cage for the nimbler class of animals in some great zoological garden. . . . a little world of bars and perches and swings for human squirrels and monkeys."[8]

It is important to note that influential citizens like James did not feel it necessary to express views like these discreetly in private correspondence but felt completely free to proclaim them openly in books, magazines, and newspapers alongside the writing of other influential citizens who declaimed about "darkies," and "pickaninnies," and "redskins," and "savages," and "Chinks," and "Japs." "What Shall We Do With The Dago?" J. Appleton Morgan asked in the title of his 1890 article about the Italian immigrants in *Popular Science Monthly*. These were not the views of extremists but those of polite society whose members were pained at the people they now had to share space with. In spite of his obvious privilege and position, James professed—and obviously really felt—himself to be displaced and rendered impotent by the new immigrants. He observed the dismally poor Jews of the Lower East Side and spoke of "the Hebrew conquest of New York." He stood on Boston's Beacon Hill one late winter Sunday afternoon in 1907 watching the crowds of strolling workers "of the simpler sort" dressed in their Sunday best and found that "no sound of English, in a single instance, escaped their lips; the greater number spoke a rude form of Italian, the others some outland dialect unknown to me. . . . No note of any shade of American speech struck my ear, . . . the people before me were gross aliens to a man, and they were in serene and triumphant possession."[9]

Seven years later, the University of Wisconsin sociologist and progressive reformer Edward Alsworth Ross also observed a group of new immigrants—Magyars, Russians, Hebrews, South Slavs, Italians, Greeks, and Portuguese—in their Sunday best and commented, "They simply look out of place in black clothes and stiff collar, since clearly they belong in skins, in wattled huts at the close of the Great Ice Age. These oxlike men are descendants of those *who always stayed behind*." The "pioneer breed" was now being "swamped and submerged" by the "Caliban type." Madison Grant, the chairman of the New York Zoological Society and a trustee of the American Museum of Natural History, charged in a widely read book in 1916 that the "maudlin sentimentalism that has made America 'an asylum for the oppressed,'" along with a "pathetic and fatuous belief in the efficacy of American

institutions and environment to reverse or obliterate immemorial
hereditary tendencies," were responsible for this new immigration
which contained "a large and increasing number of the weak, the
broken, and the mentally crippled of all races drawn from the lowest stratum of the Mediterranean basin and the Balkans, together
with hordes of the wretched, submerged populations of the Polish
ghettos." These newcomers adopted the language, wore the
clothes, stole the name of the Nordic American, "and they are
beginning to take his women, but they seldom adopt his religion
or understand his ideals." The day of the "Great Race" that had
built the United States, he lamented, was coming to a close.[10]

These Italians and Greeks and Jews and Poles and Bohemians,
whose faces on the streets of the cities he visited struck James as so
"low," and whose "alien" presence led to the birth of the Americanization movement of the early twentieth century, the rebirth of
the Ku Klux Klan in 1915, and the passage of immigration legisla-
tion aimed at curtailing their numbers in 1921 and 1924, became in
their turn paradigms of what desirable immigrants ought to be, as
Hispanics and Asians dominated the immigration of the 1980s and
1990s. There is not one argument used against contemporary
immigrants, not one dire prediction about the dismal future we
face because of their presence, not one rationale for closing the
door in their faces, that has not been aimed at earlier immigrant
groups.

African Americans figured prominently in these periodic bursts
of hysteria and despair. Shortly after the Civil War there were
euphoric predictions that Black Americans were on the threshold
of extinction. In Mississippi, the *Meridian Clarion* announced
in August 1865 that in one hundred years "the negro will be dead.
Slavery is abolished now, but in a hundred years the negro himself
will be abolished." Five months later the editor of the *Natchez
Democrat* proclaimed, "The child is already born who will behold
the last negro in the state of Mississippi. With no one to provide
for the aged and the young, the sick and the helpless incompe-
tent to provide for themselves, and brought unprepared into

competition with the superior intelligence, tact, and muscle of
free white labor, they must surely and speedily perish." In 1865 a
former slaveholder in South Carolina predicted that the ex-slaves
"will perish by hunger and disease and melt away as snow before
the rising sun," and in 1868 a *New York Times* correspondent in
that state was "solemnly impressed with the conviction that the
colored race in the South is destined to die out." As in the case of
Indians, "the darker and inferior race must go to the wall."[11]

The census of 1870, which seriously undercounted Black Americans and thus showed them declining with relation to White
Americans, gave sustenance to this view, and seemed to constitute
evidence for the prediction Charles Darwin made a year later in
his *Descent of Man:* "At some future period, not very distant . . .
the civilized races of man will almost certainly exterminate, and
replace, the savage races throughout the world." The census of
1880, however, showed a higher rate of population growth among
Blacks than Whites and swung the pendulum of prediction—and
delusion—in the opposite direction. In 1883, Dr. Edward W.
Gilliam, writing in the *Popular Science Monthly,* calculated that by
1980 there would be a Black population of 192 million: "This dark,
swelling, muttering mass along the social horizon, gathering
strength with education, and ambitious to rise, will grow increasingly restless and sullen under repression, until at length, conscious through numbers of superior power, it will assert that
power destructively, and, bursting forth like an angry furious
crowd, avenge in tumult and disorder, the social law broken
against them." In his widely read *An Appeal to Caesar,* Albion
Tourgee predicted that by 1900 *"each of the states lying between
Maryland and Texas will have a colored majority within its borders;
and we shall have eight minor republics of the Union in which either
the colored race will rule or a majority will be disfranchised."* Still
another estimate insisted that southern Blacks would increase to
fifty million by the 1950s. "The whites will be outnumbered in a
constantly increasing majority, if the black vote is counted; if

uncounted or suppressed a bloody war of the races will inevitably result."[12]

Surely, to paraphrase George Kennan, there ought to be a lesson in all of this. Surely, there is: we who inhabit the United States at this moment are not unique, nor is our situation. Every previous generation of Americans has had its profound difficulties accepting ethnic and racial groups who did not seem to adhere to some earlier model; every previous generation of Americans has spied in the new immigration of its own time the seeds of dissolution and chaos; every previous generation of Americans—composed of the children of earlier immigrants—has seen itself as the native guardians of the Pure and Original America. And every previous generation of Americans has been incorrect in its fears and its certainties because every previous generation—and our own as well—has understood only very imperfectly the phenomena of immigration and assimilation.

What we need is not further exacerbation of these deeply rooted and deeply unfortunate tendencies but further understanding of the actual nature of our society.

The Ethnic Dynamic

Contemporary predictions that the United States is in danger of being overwhelmed by an immigration of a different sort fit easily into a well-established pattern of calamity and fantasy. In the recent past, however, scholars have gone further than ever before toward forging a clearer picture of the ethnic dimension of our diversity. By 1975 Talcott Parsons had retreated from his earlier universalistic determinism and admitted that "complete assimilation leading to the disappearance of ethnic identities and solidarities" had not taken place: "Indeed, full assimilation, in the sense that ethnic identification has virtually disappeared and become absorbed within the single category of 'American,' is very little the case."[1]

Armed with perceptions like this, scholars began to probe more closely the nature of ethnic identification and assimilation. Milton Gordon, whose work on assimilation has been tremendously influential, cautioned against oversimplifying the process of assimilation by homogenizing it. He distinguished between at least two basic types of assimilation: *cultural or behavioral* assimilation which was usually rapid and widespread and entailed absorbing such cultural behavior patterns of the "host" society as language, dress, and manner, and *structural* assimilation which was much slower and less complete and consisted of entering the "structures" of the larger society—its organizations and institutions. Of course a good deal of structural assimilation was inevitable since almost all ethnic and racial groups attended the schools, worked in the factories and offices, and frequently joined the unions and the political organizations of the larger society. But their *primary* associations tended to be held within their own structures: "From the cradle in the sectarian hospital to the child's play group, the social clique in high school, the fraternity and religious center in college, the dating group within which he searches for a spouse, the marriage partner, the neighborhood of his residence, the church affiliation and the church clubs, the men's and the women's social and service organizations, the adult clique of 'marrieds,' the vacation resort, and then, as the age cycle nears completion, the rest home for the elderly and, finally, the sectarian cemetery—in all these activities and relationships which are close to the core of personality and selfhood—the member of the ethnic group may if he wishes follow a path which never takes him across the boundaries of his ethnic structural network."[a]

Although one might argue with Gordon about the precise extent of structural assimilation, his distinction is crucial and at the heart of many of our confusions. People who *look* and *act* totally assimilated to some general norm, can—and in American society often have *had* to—keep their most intimate and significant associations within their own specific group and maintain a discrete culture which lives alongside the larger culture of which they are also a part. While the outside world may perceive complete assimilation, the reality is much more complex. My own father, who emigrated to the United States in 1913 when Anglo-conformist sentiment was at its height, provides concrete evidence of Gordon's point. He learned English and rarely spoke Yiddish to his children because he wanted them to be *Americans;* became an avid baseball fan who came close to idolizing the great Yankee first baseman Lou Gehrig; dressed and groomed himself precisely like other lower-middle-class and working-class Americans; became a life-long Democrat who had difficulty voting for Congressman Jacob Javits, whose religion and liberal political views he shared, because Javits ran on the Republican ticket; was intensely proud of being a naturalized American and never understood his children's desire to someday travel abroad since the United States contained so many "wonders" worth seeing first. Yet this same man belonged until his death in 1969 to a fraternal society composed exclusively of immigrants from the little Lithuanian village of Shot where he had grown up; married the daughter of a Russian Jewish immigrant family; held and maintained many of the same Orthodox and folkish Jewish tenets as his forebears; had no close friends who were not Eastern European Jews or their descendants; lived his entire social life among those friends and his large extended family; rarely strayed far from the Jewish, Greek, Armenian, immigrant neighborhood in which we lived and in which my parents kept a "mom and pop" fruit and vegetable store in which they worked almost all the time and consequently saw few of the American scenic wonders my father spoke of with such pride; took his brief annual vacation in the "Borscht Belt" of the Catskill Mountains where he shared the countryside with still more Eastern European Jewish immigrants and their progeny; and finally was laid to rest in the midst of the same people with whom he had spent his life.

My mother, the oldest child of Russian Jewish immigrants, though she was born in New York City, spoke a purer English and had a more complete understanding of the United States than my father, never abandoned the same associational and cultural network that characterized his life and the life of her parents. Though they had their feet planted in more than one culture, neither of my parents fit the "marginal man" model which sociologists like Robert Park once argued dominated immigrant culture whose typical denizen was portrayed as "par excellence, the 'stranger,'" condemned "to live in two worlds," torn between "the warm security of the ghetto, which he has abandoned, and the cold freedom of the outer world, in which he is not yet quite at home."[3] Park, and following him the historian Oscar Handlin, certainly did not invent these conflicts; they were real and often agonizing. But he and his colleagues tended to exaggerate the need to decide between cultures, to abandon the old in order to embrace the new. They underestimated the ability of people to retain and nurture a good deal of the old even as they entered and were shaped by the new. They seem not to have comprehended adequately the extent to which the periphery could affect the center; the many ways in which the shaped could become shapers and the lineaments of the minority culture could not only be influenced by but could also influence the larger culture.

Together my parents made certain that their American-born, college-educated children imbibed the essence of the culture and the values that had defined their own lives. I was not raised in an either-or, cut-and-dried, black-or-white, this-or-that universe. I could have both Moses *and* Lincoln for forefathers, both the Hebrew Torah *and* the United States Constitution for moral and legal touchstones, both Joshua *and* Joe Louis for warrior heroes, both the Jewish *shul and* the American public school for houses of learning. I understood from early in my life that I was not expected to *choose* between cultural venues so much as to negotiate, and navigate, between them; to dwell amidst a variety of riches and understand how to accommodate them all; to learn to live with   to borrow from Du Bois—my "twoness": an American, a Jew; "two souls, two thoughts, two unreconciled strivings."

But it was even more complicated and far more multicultural than this, for the influences upon me as I grew up were not just East-European Jewish and Anglo American; they were also Greek American, Armenian American, German-Jewish American, African American, Irish American, Italian American, Chinese American. I was not only raised with kids named Hirsch, Goldman, and Handleman but also with kids named Demopolous, Cademian, Seropian, Mennona, Larrea, Gwon, and McCann. The physical and verbal games I played, the words I spoke and the dialect I spoke them in, the jokes I told, the ways I dressed and walked and held my body, the songs I sang, the folklore I heard and disseminated, the models of gender—and especially of "manhood"—I learned were not a simple mix of two separate cultures; they were the amalgam of the many disparate groups I grew up with. Each of these peripheries were shaped not merely by the center but by many of the other peripheries as well, and the center itself was altered by all of these influences to a degree none of the major paradigms of identity allowed for.

Outside of the public schools, one of my chief forays into American culture came through frequenting jazz clubs in the late 1940s when I was still in my early and mid-teens. Thus one of my earliest exposures to the larger culture outside of the familiar confines of my small world, one of my first introductions to a cultural experience my parents had never had, was the world of young Black musicians like Charlie Parker, Dizzy Gillespie, Thelonius Monk, Ella Fitzgerald, Sarah Vaughn, Billie Holiday, and Lester Young whose sessions I attended as often as I could afford to and whose innovative music became a central part of my own cultural world. One of the most important acculturative phases of my young life, then, was connected to *African* American culture. Judging from the diverse mix of people I met at the Royal Roost, Birdland, and Bop City, I was not alone.

Indeed, as I learned after I became a historian, my experience was not particularly new. In the 1920s a group of White youngsters in and around Chicago—Benny Goodman, Bud Freeman, Dave Tough, Eddie Condon, Milton "Mezz" Mezzrow, Gene Krupa, Muggsy Spanier, Jimmy McPartland, Frank Teschemacher, Joe Sullivan, George Wettling—encountered the music of such Black jazz musicians as Joe Oliver, Jimmie Noone, Johnny and Baby Dodds, and Louis Armstrong who were then playing in the clubs on Chicago's South Side. Condon recalled that he and his friends spoke about jazz "as if it were a new religion just come from Jerusalem." Here was a cultural medium that allowed these youngsters, many of whom came from immigrant and ethnic families outside the mainstream, to approach the larger society with a degree of musical and personal individuality. Hoagy Carmichael, who grew up in Indiana and became part of the Chicago group, recalled that World War I was over but the rebellion against "the accepted, the proper and the old" was just beginning. "And for us jazz articulated. . . . It said what we wanted to say though what that was we might not know." Reggie Duval, a Black pianist in Indianapolis, taught Carmichael to "never play anything that ain't *right*. You may not make any money, but you'll never get hostile with yourself." Jazz was teaching these youngsters, according to Mezzrow, to speak out in their own "honest and self-inspired language."[4]

At the end of another world war, several of my friends and I, Jewish boys from immigrant families, felt exactly the same way. Through these jazz musicians we not only found an art that touched us, we also saw the possibility of functioning in the outside society while retaining our individual and ethnic personas; *they* were doing it and we could find a means of doing it as well. To understand what happened to me and my friends and to the Chicago youth before us, one has to drop the simple model of each ethnic and racial group interacting singly on a one-to-one basis with the central "Anglo American" culture. The situation was more elaborate and involved than that; in an ethnically diverse society cultural models abounded and one had choices and influences far more numerous than many of the theorizers of assimilation and acculturation recognized.

This was certainly the lesson American scholars were deriving from their research in the very decades in which I was beginning my career in the academic world. As the United States entered the last third of the twentieth century, ethnic differentiation became as familiar as socioeconomic differentiation. "One of the unique aspects of American society," Gerard Postiglione wrote, "is its multiple pluralisms, but *the most* unique pluralism of all is the heritage of its people." Ethnicity, he concluded, "is an indispensable element in the complex equation of American culture and social structure. No American community has yet been fully explained without it." Michael Novak posited the emergence of a "pluralistic personality" which was "both more aware of others and also more aware of [its] own distinctive cultural identity."[5]

Though such social scientists as Postiglione, Novak, Milton Gordon, Nathan Glazer, Daniel Patrick Moynihan, Francis X. Femminella, and Andrew Greeley are a diverse group with a variety of arguments and approaches, it is possible to sum up one of the uniting elements in their work by employing the central concept of Nathan Glazer's and Daniel Patrick Moynihan's 1963 book, *Beyond the Melting Pot*. "The point about the melting pot," the authors announce at the beginning, "is that it did not happen." The various immigrant groups were not melted into something that already existed, were not converted to someone else's identity, were not blended "into a standard, uniform national type," but were *transformed* by influences in their new environment and *recreated* as a complex of the old and the new, that which was established and that which was still in process of becoming: not Irish *or* American, not African *or* American, not Italian *or* American, but composite groups—Irish American, African American, Italian American. Of course they were not monolithic groups; internally their members differed among themselves according to their education, their standard of living, their means of employment, their place of residence, their immediate histories. Nor were they exclusive groups; the *American* portion of their designations established important lines of continuity of language, taste, behavior, expectation. Thus they touched, influenced, and were influenced by each other on a regular basis. Finally, they were not static groups; they were simultaneously the products and the agents of change; their identities were "matters of choice as well as of heritage; of new creation in a new country, as well as of the maintenance of old values and forms." As the old immigrant culture began to dissolve, a new culture shaped by the American experience was created: "Italian-Americans might share precious little with Italians in Italy, but in America they were a distinctive group that maintained itself, was identifiable, and gave something to those who were identified with it, just as it also gave burdens that those in the group had to bear." The essential point is that in a society composed of self-conscious groups, ethnicity did not merely survive as a vestige of the past; it existed as a dynamic factor in an American identity which was itself not yet finally established. "The American nationality is still forming," Glazer and Moynihan concluded, " . . . and the final form, if there is ever to be a final form, is as yet unknown."[6]

This awareness of dynamism, of change, of interaction has dominated recent scholarship. We have rediscovered that sense of excitement, that sense of as yet unrealized possibilities that informed Emerson's, Melville's, and Turner's discussions of American identity. Scholars have finally set about exploring and amending and expanding the notions of pluralism set forth by Du Bois, Kallen, and Bourne so long ago. What has informed almost all of these discussions is a refusal to freeze American identity into a central unchanging form. White Anglo Protestant Americans, for all their importance through the years, are no longer conceived as *the* central group whose culture defines the norm. They are seen as one—albeit a very influential one—of the ethnic groups that have contributed to and helped to forge an American culture and identity which, to reiterate the point, is still in process, still being formed, still becoming.

The United States, Francis X. Femminella has asserted, received much more than just people from its cycles of immigration; it acquired an "immigrant culture" which is the key to understanding the development of the nation. Femminella refers to what he calls "emergent culture" to describe this American immigrant culture whose most salient characteristic is change itself: "Ethnic groups in this culture are not to be thought of as merely unassimilated holdouts left over from the earlier immigrations which will disappear in time. Rather they have become a fundamental part of United-Statesian social structure." Conflict is built into the pattern. Femminella employs the term "impact-integration" to symbolize this conflict and its results. "Impact" refers to the entanglement, the collision, the "boundary crisis" that occurs when newer cultures encroach upon the turf of older ones; "integration" refers to the new cultural syntheses that emerge from the impact. This integration is not invariably peaceful; it can be violent and prolonged and frequently involves exploitation and attempts at subordination. The result, Femminella argues, is not the disappearance of the newcomers but a cultural integration involving the evolution of new cultural forms in which both the newcomers and the older residents are changed. It is in this sense that the United States is always and ever an *emerging* nation.[7]

In 1987 the Swedish anthropologist Ulf Hannerz took the provocative and intriguing step of applying the idea of creolization to American culture. "Creole"—a term which with the exception of Louisiana has been generally applied to cultures in the Caribbean and Africa—refers to cultural phenomena, such as languages, "which draw in some way on two or more historical sources, often originally widely different. They have had time to develop and integrate." Hannerz argues that while creole culture is the product of center-periphery relations, it does not involve a merely passive acceptance of the central culture by the peripheral cultures; it is an open-ended process which includes crucial contributions by those cultures on the periphery to the final cultural outcome. Indeed in the United States the process has been complicated by the presence of so many different cultures and by the fact that these cultures have creolized each other as well as the central culture: "Ethnic boundaries remain noticeable, yet cultural meanings and forms flow across them." Thus, to give one example, American music with African forms and sources of inspiration is no longer exclusively confined to African American music; it includes forms of White mountain music, White church music, mainstream popular music, and varieties of symphonic music which have been highly influenced by African American music throughout our history. "Old subcultures keep reinventing themselves, and new subcultures keep being born. It is this diversity of American culture, and this continued fluidity of culture along the creolizing continuum, that many Europeans find most difficult to grasp."[8]

Hannerz may well be correct about the European failure to understand the American cultural process, but I think it's important to observe that whether they grasp the process or not, what has made America *America* to Europeans is precisely the presence and intermingling of diverse cultures into a new and often unique cultural amalgam. "America in 1992 is not the America I came to in 1966," Andrei Codrescu, who emigrated to the United States from Romania, told a group of new citizens at their swearing-in ceremony. "Millions of people from Asia, the Caribbean and the Pacific have come since then, changing the flavor and look of the place, making America more colorful, spicier, more exciting."[9] The fact is that Europeans have never mistaken us for English men and women living on the other side of the Atlantic. From Crève-coeur and Tocqueville on, they have understood us to be a distinct people with a distinct culture. Indeed, they have often understood this more clearly than many of our own would-be cultural guardians and leaders.

These scholarly formulations transport us a long way from Henry Ford's massive melting pot which took no prisoners and left no traces of those who immersed themselves in its bubbling liquids. Our ideas are currently a good deal less neat; *our* crucible is much messier and not only leaves many traces of those who pass through it but somehow changes the processors as well as the processed. On the surface this may seem like a much less comforting way to explain and understand our society and our culture. Perhaps we simply have to take comfort in the fact that the notion of the United States as a society which is constantly *emerging*, with an identity and a culture which are never permanently fixed, does seem to mirror reality much more closely than previous explanations. Indeed, contemporary explanations help clarify those very American characteristics that so excited Frederick Jackson Turner:

the sense of eternal rebirth, the ever vital process of becoming, the insistence on being free from the confines of the past, the receptivity to change and newness.

Because Turner linked these characteristics to the frontier, he grieved for his America when the frontier disappeared. But what if his tears were premature, what if this was Turner's error? Perhaps the true American frontier has not been land and space, but the *people:* those who were already here when the first Europeans and Africans came to these shores and those who have come continuously ever since. Accused of perverting the "national genius" because of his unpopular views during World War I, the German Jewish immigrant Ludwig Lewisohn asked in 1922: "But suppose *I* am the national genius?"[10] For all its intended frivolity, it was—and is—a question that deserves the most serious contemplation. The diverse peoples, who came to or were brought to America for a myriad of reasons, have proven to be a far less exhaustible resource than the land itself and may well have been the source of those very qualities that Turner—and before him Tocqueville and Emerson and Melville and Whitman—most admired and celebrated about the United States. *Their* America was not a fixed entity to which all newcomers had to adjust. It was a dynamic *becoming,* a nascent experiment to which all newcomers contributed by bringing themselves, blending their cultures, and creating something new. America was not something that *had* happened; it was continually in the process of happening—*this* was its uniqueness and its promise. Recent sociological and anthropological theories have helped to capture and explain many of these complexities.

The implications of this scholarship for American education are clear. As early as 1940 Caroline Ware and several of her colleagues criticized historians for writing studies and textbooks "primarily from the standpoint of the Anglo-Saxon myth. While we abuse the Germans for overemphasizing the Nazi myth, we continue to employ a historical myth of our own." It was no longer sufficient "to assume that American culture is the culture of the old-American, Anglo-Saxon group," or to write American history exclusively from the "Plymouth Rock" view. "Immigrants and the children of immigrants," they insisted, *are* the American people. Their culture *is* American culture, not merely a contributor to American culture."[11] If we add to this insight the Native American and Hispanic peoples who were already here when the United States incorporated their lands, and those African Americans who came not as immigrants but as slaves, it would stand as a good description of what has been one of the primary interests of recent historians: the relationship of the discrete ethnic cultures to "American" culture.

Fifty years later, in her 1990 presidential address to the Modern Language Association, Catharine R. Stimpson defined multiculturalism as "the necessary recognition that we cannot think of culture unless we think of many cultures at the same time."[12] The problem, of course, is that most of the many cultures that have existed in the United States have been neglected or ignored by historians and before we can think about them "at the same time," we first have to study and understand them. This has been one of the major tasks of recent historiography which has done more than all previous generations of historians combined to penetrate the darkness that has surrounded the dynamic history of the individual racial and ethnic groups in the United States.

Explanations

Perhaps the most important intellectual breakthrough by historians in the past few decades has been their changed attitude toward the folk whom *Webster's New International Dictionary* defined as "the masses of people of lower culture" but whom scholars now began to see in a very different light: Not as inarticulate, impotent, irrelevant historical ciphers continually processed by forces over which they had no control but rather as actors in their own right who, to a larger extent than we previously imagined, were able to build a culture, create alternatives, affect the situation they found themselves in, and influence the people they found themselves among.

One hundred years ago William James wrote of being in the mountains of North Carolina and seeing what at first appeared to be pure squalor: settlers had killed all the trees, planted their crops around the stumps, and erected their rough cabins and crude fences, thus marring the landscape. "The forest," James observed, "had been destroyed; and what had 'improved' it out of existence was hideous, a sort of ulcer, without a single element of artificial grace to make up for the loss of Nature's beauty. Ugly indeed seemed the life of the squatter." But greater acquaintance with the people of the area taught him his error:

> When *they* looked on the hideous stumps, what they thought of was personal victory. The chips, the girdled trees and the vile split rails spoke of honest sweat, persistent toils and final reward. The cabin was a warrant of safety for self and wife and babes. In short, the clearing, which to me was a mere ugly picture on the retina, was to them a symbol redolent with moral memories and sang a very paean of duty, struggle, and success.

"I had been . . . blind to the peculiar ideality of their conditions," James concluded. He attributed this to what he called the "ancestral blindness" of his own class which troubled him deeply: "We of the highly educated classes (so called) . . . are trained to seek the choice, the rare, the exquisite, exclusively, and to overlook the common. We are stuffed with abstract conceptions, and glib with verbalities and verbosities; and in the culture of these higher functions . . . we grow stone-blind and insensible to life's more elementary and general goods and joys." Significance, James complained, "lies all about us, and culture is too hidebound to even suspect the fact."[1]

James's insights help define the directions in which the study of history has moved in the past few decades. In the title card to his 1919 silent film *True Heart Susie*, D. W. Griffith asked: "Is real life interesting?"[2] Though they often compressed the realities of life into the shorthand of melodrama, Griffith and his fellow filmmakers, especially in the early decades of their craft, answered this question with a resounding "Yes!" It has taken historians and other scholars a good deal longer to come to the same conclusion. By our own time, they have finally made this discovery, and *everyday* life and thought have become a legitimate part of the subject matter pursued by scholars and students.

In a seminar I taught for Berkeley history majors during the spring of 1994, I asked the students to read *The Surrounded*, a 1936 novel by D'Arcy McNickle, a Native American writer

from the Salish people of Montana. In her written reflections on
McNickle's work, one of my students, Marie Valgos, manifested
her grasp of the changes that were transforming American education: "It is a shame that such a moving and heartfelt book
would have to wait fifty-some years to gain an appreciative audience. I am happy to be a student in an era when not just one but
many voices teach history." Those of us fortunate enough to
have written, taught, or studied history during the past several
decades have been free as never before to move into neighborhoods once blocked to scholars, teachers, and students, to learn
from people previously invisible to us, to study subjects once
thought beneath us, to take into account the heterogeneity and
complexity of our society.

By reaching out and making our craft more inclusive and complete than it has ever been before, historians have created an exciting period of growth and discovery in which many cultural
assumptions, often based more on prejudices than careful study,
are being overturned or rethought. In the last few decades we
have begun to study women, immigrants, workers, slaves, lesbians
and gays, children, Native Americans, African, Asian, and Hispanic Americans, Eastern and Southern European Americans, and
indeed Northern and Western European Americans as well, for
what we're talking about is not simply ethnicity or gender but
power, and the ignored and the neglected have included untold
millions of White Anglo-Saxon Protestant American women and
men whom scholarly neglect had reduced to historical ciphers.
We are breathing life back into the history of people we had allowed to disappear from our consciousness. The result has been
exhilarating.

The exhilaration over the rediscovery of neglected peoples has
not been confined to the scholarly world, as the reaction to the
Vietnam Veterans Memorial attests, but neither has it been universal. The serious historical examination of the culture and the activities of those long considered to be insignificant appears to many
in and outside the academe to be trivial pursuits. In his 1968

presidential address, Thomas A. Bailey warned the Organization of American Historians that historians should be wary of the increasing clamor among Blacks for "historical recognition" since "the luckless African-Americans while in slavery were essentially in jail; and we certainly would not write the story of a nation in terms of its prison population." In 1982 Professor C. Vann Woodward of Yale University denounced what he perceived to be the shift of focus from "the elites and the powerful" to "the family, the nursery, the bedroom, the deathbed . . . marriage, birth rates and sex roles; to popular culture; to the history of prisons, hospitals, villages, cities and churches." He insisted that "people of a democratic tradition can surely be interested in the historic plight of the powerless, but they have a natural and abiding concern for power and those who have wielded it and to what effect."[3]

Similarly, in her 1987 book *The New History and the Old,* the historian Gertrude Himmelfarb grumbled about the "current prejudice against greatness." She complained that attention to social and cultural history devalues political history by denying "that man is the distinctive, indeed unique animal Aristotle thought him to be—a rational animal, which is to say a political animal." She charged that social historians rejected "any such 'elitist' idea as the good life, seeking only to understand *any* life, indeed regarding it as a triumph of the historical imagination to explore the lowest depths of life." We are in serious danger, she concluded, of losing "the notable events, individuals, and institutions that have constituted our historical memory and our heritage."[4] Too much interest in the people and their culture, it seemed, was like that fatal first glass of beer the prohibitionists used to warn about: it made it impossible for one to experience and appreciate the higher things in life.

Skepticism about the value of studying the history of the American people in all their complexity stems from the critics' tendency to equate the history of plain people and their cultures with the history of "victims." In fact, the contemporary historical focus is most often the opposite, not on suffering and powerlessness—

though these are certainly ingredients when they are relevant—
but on how people lived, and coped, and even occasionally tri-
umphed; on the cultures they helped to create and enjoy; on the
criteria they established by which they judged themselves and
those around them. Professor Woodward and his fellow critics
have ignored the multifaceted realities of the new scholarship and
have invented instead a one-dimensional caricature which they
never tire of attacking. Thus Woodward has complained of an
"obsession with guilt" under whose driving force "American history becomes primarily a history of oppression." The implication
is that the only thing that could possibly interest scholars in those
Woodward calls the "powerless" is their suffering, not their culture and their lives. Other critics who enjoy slogans more than
accuracy employ the term "oppression studies" to characterize the
eclectic and revealing studies of the American people which have
graced recent scholarship.[5]

To accuse contemporary historians of having abandoned politics and other "significant" subjects in favor of parochial, politically correct areas is to have seriously misread the scholarship of
the last few decades. A far more accurate assessment of the contemporary historical scene has been made in the historiographical
essays commissioned and published by the American Historical
Association and collected in *The New American History* (1990),
edited by Eric Foner, who concludes:

> Despite the apparent ascendancy of social history, these
> essays do not lend credence to recent complaints that histori-
> ans are no longer concerned with politics, economics, the
> Constitution, and intellectual history. Such traditional con-
> cerns appear in virtually every essay, although often in forms
> that earlier historians might find unrecognizable. The old
> "presidential synthesis"—which understood the evolution of
> American society chiefly via presidential elections and admin-
> istrations—is dead (and not lamented). And politics now
> means much more than the activities of party leaders.[6]

The assertion that there are powerless groups of people who don't deserve our attention because they are in some kind of prison, some sort of apolitical limbo, from which they can exert no influence has been disproved over and over in study after study. The notion that when we write the social, cultural, and intellectual history of African Americans, immigrants, women, and workers, we are somehow writing apolitical history, abstracts politics from ordinary existence. We need to constantly remember that everyday life always intrudes on politics, always intermeshes with it, always constitutes the background for it. When we forget that, we lose the very substance of reality *and* of politics. I don't conceive of my study of slaves and their descendants as an apolitical study of the powerless. Blacks during and after slavery were engaged in the most serious game of politics and exerted power of many kinds— especially cultural power, the importance of which we are just now beginning to appreciate.

While I was writing *Black Culture and Black Consciousness* I read Robert Louis Stevenson's essay "The Lantern Bearers" (1892), in which Stevenson described how he and his schoolmates used to place a bull's eye lantern under the greatcoats they wore in the cold weather—its presence unknown to all but one another. Thus equipped, each boy would walk through the night "a mere pillar of darkness" to ordinary eyes, but each exulting in the knowledge that he had a hidden lantern shining at his belt. For Stevenson this scene of boyhood bliss became a paradigm for the human condition. A good part of reality, Stevenson wrote, "runs underground. The observer (poor soul, with his documents!) is all abroad. For to look at the man is but to court deception. . . . To one who has not the secret of the lanterns, the scene upon the links is meaningless. And hence the haunting and truly spectral unreality of realistic books."[7]

That wonderful phrase—"the haunting and truly spectral unreality of realistic books"—particularly affected me. How many "realistic" volumes of American history had I read that lacked any knowledge whatever of the "secret of the lanterns" and treated the vast majority of Americans as objects rather than subjects, lacking any culture worthy of close or sustained examination. Group after group has walked through American history with their cultural lanterns obscured from the uncomprehending eyes of outside observers. *This* is the vast gap in our past that so many scholars have been trying to fill.

I know personally how complex and rewarding this attempt can be. While I was writing my first book, a study of the politician William Jennings Bryan, I became increasingly interested in the culture of his followers, those rural and small-town White Protestant southerners and westerners whom Bryan championed from the 1890s to the 1920s, but I was unsure about how to get at their culture directly and tended to let Bryan speak for them.

When the Bryan book was published, I began a study of Black protest thought in the twentieth century and set to work reading the writings of African American leaders from W. E. B. Du Bois to Stokely Carmichael. I soon realized that I was falling into the same pattern of allowing the leadership to speak for their followers. It is undeniably crucial to pay attention to leaders, but as an exclusive approach it is also undeniably limited. It was certainly no way to uncover "the personal poetry, . . . the rainbow work of fancy" that Stevenson insisted lay hidden within human beings. This time around I was determined to find ways to give voice to people who had been rendered historically inarticulate by historians who concentrated on a relatively narrow spectrum of written sources and thus transformed the American people into what Ralph Ellison called "the void of faceless faces, of soundless voices lying outside history." "We, who write no novels, histories or other books," the protagonist of Ellison's novel *Invisible Man* muses. "What about us?" It was a question that began to engross me.[8]

To respond to this question was not solely a technical matter of finding the right sources; it was also and perhaps primarily an intellectual and cultural matter of overcoming a host of attitudes and prejudices that stood in the way. We were told over and over, for instance, that African Americans had either a vacuum or a

sickness where culture should have been. *"American Negro culture,"* the influential scholar Gunnar Myrdal insisted in italics, ". . .
*is a distorted development, or a pathological condition, of the general
American culture,"* and the psychologists Abram Kardiner and
Lionel Ovesey wrote in 1951 that at the time of emancipation the
freedman "had no culture, . . . no pride, no group solidarity,
no tradition," a condition from which "he has never since freed
himself."[9]

Happily, there were other voices pointing in other directions if
only one paid attention. "In all the books that you have studied
you never have studied Negro history have you?" an ex-slave asked
an interviewer from Fisk University. "If you want Negro history
you will have to get [it] from somebody who wore the shoe, and
by and by from one to the other you will get a book."[10] Of course,
many different kinds of Black people "wore the shoe" during and
after slavery and no one body of sources could speak for them all.
Nevertheless, the materials of African American oral culture—
songs, tales, folk beliefs, jokes, reminiscences, toasts, anecdotes—
give voice to that very large segment of the Black community
about whom we have known the least.

Once I began to explore the expressive culture of the Black
folk, I found it so rich and rewarding that ultimately it took over
the book which was almost imperceptibly transformed from a
study of the protest thought of the leadership into a study of folk
thought and culture. It turned out that I was only one of a number of historians who were moving in similar directions. The result
of all this intellectual ferment was a very different picture of the
African American past.

From the first African captives, through the years of slavery, and
into the present century, Black Americans kept alive important
strands of African consciousness and verbal art in their religious
and secular culture. They were able to do this because culture is
far more persistent and resistant to rapid change than many scholars assumed; because southern Whites found it easier to justify the
enslavement of a people different than themselves and so were

not anxious to see their Black slaves completely acculturate; and because in such areas as music and folk religion there were important parallels between Europe and Africa, allowing for cultural blending and fusion between Europeans and Africans.

The notion that American slavery transformed Africans into passive and atomized beings could not be sustained once we began to actually listen to the voices of the slaves themselves. In the large body of slave spirituals there is no trace of the message White ministers incessantly preached from the Epistles of Paul: Slaves, obey your masters. Although they were kept largely illiterate, slaves found ways to embrace those books of the Bible most meaningful and functional for them. They based many of their religious songs on the Book of Exodus and its story of the enslavement and liberation of the Children of Israel in Egypt. "And the God dat lived in Moses' time is jus' de same today," they assured themselves. Thus they could sing of oppression and of freedom not only among themselves but in the presence of their masters. They drew implications from any episode in the Scriptures that applied to them. "O my Lord delivered Daniel," they sang, "O why not deliver me, too?" The slaves took their owners' religion and made it their own not only in terms of content but also in terms of style. The *ways* in which slaves sang, moved, and danced in and out of church left no doubt at all about the extent to which they were able to amalgamate African cultures with the cultures they encountered in the United States. Indeed, the debate about whether slaves retained a sense of community is put to rest by the communal nature of their music. There was almost no solo music in slavery; slaves sang in call-and-response fashion, a distinctly African form of music. Because they refashioned significant elements of their traditional culture into an *African* American culture, slaves did not merely mimic European Americans but constituted a cultural influence of their own which had an impact upon wide areas of American expressive culture.

Once we listen to the voices of the slaves themselves our picture of their history is revised substantially. But not only of *their* history. Contrary to the claims that paying scholarly attention to the distinct groups in America has a fragmenting effect, the study of a single group has much to teach us about the entire society. The African American relationship to the larger culture suggests that the old notion of acculturation as a relentless movement in one direction is in need of revision. Blacks shared with a number of other ethnic minorities a deep ambivalence about losing themselves in mainstream American culture. When Black Americans developed the blues in the late nineteenth and early twentieth centuries, it represented the first African American music in the United States to be dominated by the individual persona of the singer. From the beginning the blues was marked by what Abbe Niles referred to as "the element of *self*"; the song centered upon the singer's feelings, experiences, fears, dreams, acquaintances, problems, idiosyncrasies. In all of these respects the blues represented not so much a new form of music as a new form of self-conception and signaled an important degree of acculturation into the larger American society with its focus upon the individual and individual expression. But the *musical* style of the blues with its emphasis upon improvisation, its polyrhythmic effects, and its methods of vocal production, tied it to traditional roots at the very moment when the migration of Blacks throughout the country and the rise of mass culture could have spelled the demise of a distinctive African American musical style. The blues illustrates the way in which a group could surge outward into the larger society while *simultaneously* revitalizing aspects of its traditional culture. Among Black Americans assimilation was not a simple one-way affair; it was a reciprocal process that resulted in an ongoing dialogue which changed but nevertheless maintained the distinctness of all the cultures involved. The Black experience alone should prompt us to reevaluate the entire image and theory of the melting pot and the ways in which various groups have related to American culture.[11]

Historians have been finding voices in a wide array of sources from immigrant newspapers to court records and trial transcripts, from popular entertainment to census reports, from photographs to the records of labor unions and fraternal organizations. All of these voices help us explain what people are and have been, and explanations, as we learned earlier, can complicate simple pictures. For some critics the complications are too much to bear. It is revealing that they have not challenged contemporary scholarship with research studies of their own, which is the way the historical debate used to be conducted. Rather, their arguments have emphasized the *focus* of contemporary historians upon neglected groups of people as well as on folk and popular culture, which the critics claim has Balkanized and trivialized our understanding of the United States, deprived us of the "wholistic" sense of the past we once had, and confused the general public which finds the new history too complex to comprehend.

But the fact that historical analysis may be complex is not evidence that it's wrong. We first heard charges of complexity not in the discipline of history but in that of physics. During the 1920s the *New York Times* published a series of editorials bitterly lamenting the fact that educated people could no longer grasp those theories on the cutting edge of science. "What common folk must be content to do in regard to Dr. Einstein," the *Times* concluded reluctantly in 1921, "is to accept the judgment of experts on his work." The *Times* seemed loath to heed its own advice and continued to return to the problem throughout the decade, always with the same pessimistic results. In a 1928 editorial entitled "A Mystic Universe," the *Times* proclaimed, "We can only hope for dim enlightenment. The situation is all the harder on the public because physics has become unintelligible precisely in an age when the citizen is supposed to be under the moral obligation to try to understand everything."[12]

History of course is not physics, and historians neither can nor want to claim the level of complexity and abstraction attained by Einstein and his colleagues. Nonetheless, historians today are engaged in a similar debate centering on matters of synthesis, complexity, and accessibility because our discipline doesn't inhabit a planet apart from the sciences; we are part of the same cultural matrix out of which the new scientific attitudes and approaches have sprung. "The new physics," the *Times* complained, "comes perilously close to proving what most of us cannot believe; at least until we have rid ourselves completely of established notions and forms of thought."[13] Much of contemporary historiography invites us to rid ourselves of established notions and to stretch our imaginations in similar ways.

Contemporary historians have demonstrated again and again that in penetrating the culture of a group they often find more than they bargained for. What looked like a group becomes an amalgam of groups; what looked like a culture becomes a series of cultures. Americans on the eve of World War II, for instance, might have seen only a monolith when they looked at Japanese Americans, but historians must see something vastly more complicated: the *Issei* born in Japan and legally barred from becoming United States citizens; the *Nisei*, born and raised here and thus citizens by birth; the *Kibei*, born here but raised in Japan and thus legally Americans and culturally Japanese; as well as those who lived in cities and those who lived on farms; those who struggled to maintain the old ways and those who hungered for acculturation. Precisely the same thing is true of every other group. "When I first came to New York," Michael Novak has recalled, "general schemes like 'Jews' shattered in my hands. I wasn't prepared for Jewish cab drivers or Jewish poverty; not for militantly conservative Jews in a teachers' union; not for countless factions, classes, political views, and neatly elaborate hierarchies of status."[14] The complexity historians deal with, then, is not the complexity of specialized languages or esoteric methodologies but the complexity of people and the cultures they create.

Because of its diverse character, the United States is a particularly intricate society and scholars have to be equally diverse and intricate in their approaches to its history. There can be no meaningful political or economic history of labor or industry in the United States without understanding the cultures and social structures of the urban-industrial working class. Since the vast majority of industrial workers at the turn of the century were immigrant and Black, they will remain a mystery to us until we study the immigrant and African American cultures from which they came. Similarly, we study the history of women not because some politically correct dogma mandates it, or because we want to provide a "feel good" therapy for women, but because we *have* to study it in order to understand our society and our culture which we simply cannot do so long as we continue the practice of virtually ignoring the history of at least half of our population as if their sex rendered them somehow historically irrelevant. To study race, ethnicity, class, and gender, then, is not political correctness, it is a historiographical necessity. Of course there is a danger of fragmenting every group we study to the point where generalizations become impossible. But there is the even greater danger— which we have suffered from during most of our history—of generalizing the things we study right out of their complexity and thus dooming to futility any attempt to truly understand our past and our present.

Historians, of course, have a good deal to do with the reception of the history we write and teach. If we tell people continually that history is invariably narrative storytelling about those whose power, position, and influence are palpable then that is precisely what they will expect from us. But this is only one form of history, and it is incumbent upon historians to inform the public, by deed and word, that there is no preferred form for the writing of history and that no single group in history and no one aspect of the past—the social, the political, the cultural, the economic—is inherently more essential or relevant than the others. If we have respect for our audience, then we must realize that they are not strangers to ambiguity and paradox. People know these things are part of life and they certainly can be taught to see them as part of history. People also know their own lives have meaning and value, and there is no reason why historians cannot help them perceive the value and meaning of the past lives of people like—and unlike—themselves.

Unfortunately, these are hard lessons to get across in the present climate when the university and scholarship are being criticized by so many who have so little time or tolerance for explanations.

Multiculturalism: Historians, Universities, and the Emerging Nation

Critics of the contemporary university have maintained that for too many professors there is no longer any "objective" truth; everything has become subjective. "An increasingly influential view," Lynn Cheney charged in 1992, "is that there is no truth to tell: What we think of as truth is merely a cultural construct, serving to empower some and oppress others. Since power and politics are part of every quest for knowledge—so it is argued—professors are perfectly justified in using the classroom to advance political agendas."[1]

Actually, what a number of scholars have argued is that because we read any text from a particular perspective and with certain questions in mind, our reading is inevitably selective. If we think of the American past as a text, any reading of U.S. history will be conditioned by who is reading the text and what is transpiring in the society at the time. This has always been the case. George Bancroft, James Ford Rhodes, Henry Adams, Frederick Jackson Turner, Charles Beard, and their peers, were all conditioned in their reading of the text of the American past by who they were, by what was going on in their times, by the prism through which they chose to look at the past. This is no less—and no more—true of contemporary historians, many of whom are looking at the American past through the prism of its constituent peoples and cultures, and are finally taking up, implicitly at least, the challenge of such hypotheses as cultural pluralism, creolization, and America's emerging nationality.

The importance of this development cannot be diminished by arguing that nonetheless Western European civilization has been the dominant form of culture in this country and thus we must pay the lion's share of attention to it. This refers only to origins. Western Europe was indisputably the point of origin of some of our most influential national values, attitudes, practices, and institutions. But as anyone who studies culture seriously should know, the point of origin is only part of the story; it has to be balanced by a comprehension of what happened to the values, practices, and institutions after they arrived. For they came not to an empty continent but to a peopled one; they came not to a homogeneous land but to an increasingly diverse one. Nor is it accurate to speak of "Western European" culture as if it were a unified whole when in fact it comprised a host of different peoples and a *series* of cultures—languages, religions, nationalities, worldviews, political systems, folkways—that often were in tension with and ran counter to one another. Thus it is simply not sufficient to speak about Western European culture, which was really a heterogeneous complex of related cultures, as if it continued to exist in some pristine form once it arrived in the United States. George Kennan writes darkly that if we examine "our great-city ghettos or the cities of Miami and Los Angeles" we will find "real and extensive cultural changes," as if he is describing something new and disturbing.[2] In fact, he is merely stating a truth that has characterized our country from the beginning, as the seventeenth- and eighteenth-century Massachusetts Puritans were among the first to discover when they failed dismally in their every effort to keep their "City on a Hill" pure and free from the influences of the many other peoples streaming into New England whose coming brought about "real and extensive cultural changes."

We must stop talking about *dominance* and *purity* and begin thinking about *transformations*. Western European cultures and institutions were transformed in the United States because they interacted with and affected each other and also came into close contact with peoples from other cultures who brought with them their own values, attitudes, and practices. Out of that ongoing contact cultural transformations took—and are still taking—place which define *American* culture.

At its core, then, multiculturalism as a historical approach means that to understand American culture it is not enough to understand only one of its components, no matter how important it may have been. It is crucial to study and understand as many of the contributing cultures and their interactions with one another as possible, not as a matter of "therapeutic" history, as the opponents of multiculturalism keep insisting, not to placate or flatter minority groups and make them feel good, as they also assert, but as a simple matter of *understanding* the nature and complexities of American culture and the processes by which it came, and continues to come, into being. There is no conflict between multiculturalism and the study of Western European culture, which itself is a product of multiculturalism as the various peoples of Western Europe met and interacted on American soil. This relatively new European amalgam cannot stand alone; it must be studied alongside the cultures of all the parts of the world that contributed significant numbers of people to the United States: Africa, Asia, Latin America, the Caribbean, and the non-Western parts of Europe. Historians have been interested not only in uncovering the history of the many groups which have comprised the United States but also in illuminating the process by means of which, in Francis X. Femminella's words, "a synthesis occurs which unites but does not homogenize the groups."[3]

But it is not enough to study the various components of American society and culture, historians have to *explain* clearly why they're doing so. When I attended the City College of New York in the early 1950s, I lived at home with my parents and I now sometimes wonder what they would have thought if instead of bringing home history assignments concerning ancient Greece, Elizabethan England, or Puritan America—subjects my parents knew little about but whose legitimacy as "learning" they recognized—I had returned with work concerning the East-European Jewish *shtetls* and American immigrant neighborhoods from which my family had come and in which they continued to live. Would they have been pleased or would they have wondered what kind of bizarre education their son was getting? Insofar as parents, and others, are asking the latter question today, it's because historians and other academics have done a poor job of defining themselves and their work to the public and often even to their own students. We have been more guilty of political ineptitude than of political correctness.

Recent historical studies have begun to examine how ethnicity interacts with class, have studied the Old World cultures from which the various ethnic groups originated, and have begun to transcend an exclusively American orientation by placing immigration and ethnicity within a more comparative framework. These studies have continued the shift away from the once-dominant assimilation model and through careful analysis of ethnic culture they have uncovered patterns of both ethnic adaptation and ethnic revitalization. They have not dealt with immigrants as a single group but have paid close attention to such contexts as when, how, and from where ethnic groups came to the United States, the economic, social, and political conditions in which they lived, and how these factors influenced their development and affected their interactions with other groups in the United States. They have discovered that ethnicity functions as a resource which the immigrants use to cope with the environment and in this sense ethnicity itself often becomes a means of adapting to the host society. They have studied ethnic groups from within, through a close reading of their cultures, and they have broadened their studies to include such neglected components of the community as women and children, such ignored areas as the home and the workplace,

and such formerly invisible subjects as patterns of leisure and popular culture. Above all, they have paid attention to the ways in
which the people they study were able to affect their own lives. As
the historian John Bodnar has concluded about immigrants and
their progeny: "Their lives were not entirely of their own making,
but they made sure that they had something to say about it."[4]

To be sure, all the contemporary scholars who have studied
these areas are by no means unanimous in their assessment of the
issues I have raised here. John Higham has complained of "the
idealization of ethnicity in so much current scholarship," and of
the tendency to fragment rather than unify our history; David
Hollinger urges us to join him in exploring the contours of a
"postethnic America"; Gary Nash wants multiculturalism "to get
beyond a promiscuous pluralism that gives every thing equal
weight," and "reach some agreement on what is at the core of
American culture"; Werner Sollors's concerns are articulated in a
book entitled: *Beyond Ethnicity;* Henry Louis Gates, Jr., warns
that "the mindless celebration of difference has proven as unten-
able as that bygone model of monochrome homogeneity" and
calls for greater balance; Michael Omi and Howard Winant dissent strongly from what they call "the dominant ethnicity paradigm," insist upon "the *centrality of race* in American society,"
and criticize their colleagues for trying "to pound the square peg
of race into the round hole of ethnicity." Such constructive and
informed critiques create the basis for an exciting and fruitful
debate that will sharpen our inquiry into the nature of American
identity, diversity, and commonality.[5]

But this debate will not be furthered by those who either mis-
represent the rich and pioneering scholarship of the past several
decades or have simply learned nothing from it. "I think the
notion of a hyphenated American is un-American," the historian
and former Librarian of Congress Daniel Boorstin has announced.
"I believe there are only *Americans.* Polish-Americans, Italian-
Americans or African-Americans are an emphasis that is not
fertile." The question, of course, is not whether such categories

are "fertile" but whether they exist and function in the real world, whether, that is, they reflect reality. Arthur Schlesinger, Jr., speaks of "the brittle bonds of national identity that hold this diverse and fractious society together," and maintains that the United States faces a choice between polar opposites: *either* one believes in the idea of "one people" or one is contributing to the "disintegration of the national community, apartheid, Balkanization, tribalization." Again, there is no sense that a national society can live and thrive while containing disparate ethnic communities and a denial that this has in fact been the case throughout our history: "Most Americans . . . continue to see themselves primarily as individuals and only secondarily and trivially as adherents of a group," Schlesinger insists. Community, Boorstin asserts, should be our goal: "an emphasis on what brings us together—is what I think is called for in our time."[6]

It's difficult to see how community is fostered by condemning pluralism as "un-American" and ignoring all the evidence we have of the complex and multiple ways in which people in our country envision themselves and others even as they manage to create a common culture that thrives alongside the many discrete separate cultures that have characterized the United States from its origins. Community has to be built on what exists, not what some of us would like to exist.

Joseph Papp, the late theatrical producer who brought free Shakespeare and much else to the people of New York City, told the *New York Times*, "My father was a Polish Jew, I'm an American Jew or I'm a Jewish American, whichever way you put it. Sometimes I'm just a Jew. But I'm never just an American. It's impossible because there's always a sense that you're an alien." Similar thoughts were articulated more ironically in Glenn Ligon's 1992 etching featuring black print on white paper repeating the phrase I DO NOT ALWAYS FEEL COLORED over and over and over, filling the entire page as the text gets increasingly blurred and difficult to decipher at the end. Complex attitudes like these, which are far from uncommon, will never be understood through the kind of essentialism and patriotic fundamentalism too many critics of multiculturalism indulge in. They need to be read with the sophistication exhibited by David Potter who observed that some of his fellow historians too easily envision "national loyalty as if it were exclusive, and inconsistent with other loyalties," when in fact "national loyalty flourishes not by challenging and overpowering all other loyalties, but by subsuming them all in a mutually supportive relation to one another."[7]

The most disturbing aspect of many of the most prominent critiques is that they are written in a historiographical vacuum. Arthur Schlesinger, Jr., exclaims in wonder that unless one yields "to biological determinism . . . it is hard to see what living connection exists between American blacks today and their heterogeneous West African ancestors three centuries ago." But it is not especially "hard" if one reads the rich historical literature which demonstrates carefully that Africans, like Europeans—who also came from quite heterogeneous cultures—brought important elements of their Old World cultures to the New World and forged them into an *African* American culture which has certainly changed over the centuries but which continues to exist and continues to affect both Black and White Americans. This is not conjecture or politics; it is meticulously documented scholarship, and if other scholars disagree they have an obligation to alter or refute it in their own carefully researched studies, not to write as if this work had never been written.[8]

Too much of this criticism has been marked by an assaultive and ungenerous defensiveness when the United States and Western civilization are compared to other cultures. African cultures, Schlesinger tells us, are based on "despotism, superstition, tribalism, and fanaticism." The "principal offerings" of "Central African culture," the philosopher Lewis S. Feuer wrote recently, have been "disease and massacre." Similarly, the celebrated historian Hugh Trevor-Roper, in defense of what he termed "Europacentric" history, advised those undergraduates who were asking for courses in African history that "there is none, or very little:

there is only the history of the Europeans in Africa. The rest is largely darkness, like the history of pre-European, pre-Columbian America. And darkness is not a subject for history." History was interested only in "purposive movement" not "the unrewarding gyrations of barbarous tribes in picturesque but irrelevant corners of the globe." It is precisely because such educated men apparently know so little about non-Western cultures—about their art, religion, music, folklore, history, philosophy, and society—and are not only not embarrassed to display their ignorance publicly but want to *spread* it, that we desperately need a broader and deeper and more eclectic curriculum for our students.[9]

Just when a significant number of historians have begun to study the intricacies of race, ethnicity, class, and gender, just when they are beginning to penetrate the intriguing and difficult questions that the various pluralist hypotheses have posed, just when they are entering into constructive debates on these issues with their colleagues and students, others are crying that the sky is falling and that *any* deviation from the strict assimilationist melting-pot orthodoxy spells the end of the Republic as we have known it. The results of the new historiography have dismayed critics who don't like the message and all too humanly have wanted to kill the messenger, or more accurately to denounce the messenger as "politically correct." They don't mount a scholarly campaign against this work; they don't attempt to disprove it with their own scholarship; they simply denounce it as "politically correct" and "injurious" to the national tradition, as "trivial" distractions from the essential political and diplomatic work of historians. Too often they ignore the work itself and create the specter of a multiculturalism that is little more than separatism dominated by Afrocentrists and others who would stand Eurocentrism on its head and substitute still another theory of racial and ethnic superiority—this time emanating from Africa—for those doctrines of European superiority which have bedeviled us throughout our history. This is not to deny that there are theories of racial separation and superiority on all sides of the political spectrum which pose problems for the nation's schools and colleges as they always have done. But it *is* to deny strongly that such theories typify what is happening in contemporary education or that multiculturalism means ethnic separation or exclusivity. The critics of current scholarship have gotten one thing very wrong: social and racial and ethnic fragmentation are not the result of the new historiography; rather, the new historiography is, in part, a *response* to the continuing fragmentation in America which has led many scholars to question and rethink the old formulas and explanations and to look more closely at the groups that compose the United States.

At the close of his recent book, *The Disuniting of America,* Arthur Schlesinger, Jr., quotes one of his favorite historical spokesmen, the French immigrant Hector St. John Crèvecoeur, who in answering his own question: "What then is the American, this new man?" proclaimed: "Here individuals of all nations are melted into a new race of men." To which Professor Schlesinger adds, "Still a good answer—still the best hope."[10] Schlesinger is acting here as both a historian and a prophet. "Still a good answer," is a historical assessment and, judging from recent scholarship, not a very astute one; serious historical studies throughout the spectrum of American social and cultural history have demonstrated that however useful the model of the melting pot may be in understanding how assimilation and identity have worked in American history, it is not useful as a *unitary* model or paradigm—as a total answer. It does not come close to explaining the entire process to us and with it as our only guide we are doomed to only a partial understanding of our own past and present.

Indeed, Crèvecoeur's own history should give us some pause. While he may have promulgated the idea of a new race springing up on American soil and while he rhetorically denounced "ancient prejudices and manners," he himself refused either to melt or totally disavow his own "ancient prejudices and manners" and finally made his way back to the land of his origin and nativity where he presumably reverted to the French language and culture. Indeed, the paradoxical phenomenon of one of the most often quoted creators of the melting-pot hypothesis repatriating to his native land and culture may well stand as an excellent symbol of the problems inherent in the very creed Crèvecoeur was promulgating: its virtues as an ideal were not matched by its substance as a reality. All of this, of course, is debatable on historical grounds. But when Schlesinger announces that Crèvecoeur's ideas are "still the best hope," he is assuming the role not of the historian but the prophet, just as Kallen did when he pronounced cultural pluralism to be the democratic salvation for the United States. Historians have as much right as anyone else to assert their own chosen vision of the future, but they, above all, have to take special care not to confuse their hopes for tomorrow with their understanding of yesterday—a trap from which there is no easy return.

Equally seductive and perilous is the trap of the Assumed Truth. Certain ideas become so deeply ingrained, so taken for granted, that they don't seem like ideas at all but part of the Natural Order. When someone comes along who both perceives and *treats* them as ideas, subject to the challenges all ideas should be exposed to, it's as if reason itself were being challenged. The notion of the melting pot—that great crucible of the American environment swallowing, nurturing, transforming—and the notion of American culture as primarily an extension of Northern and Western Europe, came to assume this aura of the Natural Order. Any challenges, no matter how scholarly and carefully rooted in the sources and the normal rules of historical discourse, have been seen by many as assaults on rationality. It's this that accounts for the ease with which critics lump scholarly and non-scholarly, carefully researched and primarily rhetorical challenges together. Certainly, too many of the books critical of the academic world—including those by scholars—take few, if any, pains to make such distinctions; they simply dismiss *all* challenges to orthodoxy as "politically correct" and therefore worthy of no credence or careful examination.

We should heed the calls for a new synthesis but let us make certain that it is a *new* synthesis which encompasses the scholarship of the past several decades. In the essay he wrote just before his death, Nathan Huggins called for a new "Master Narrative" of American history which would replace the old narrative rooted in what he called the Founding Fathers' "avoidance of the inescapable paradox: a free nation, inspired by the Rights of Man, having to rest on slavery." Their refusal to confront and acknowledge this paradox, Huggins insisted, was "a bad way to start. It encouraged the belief that American history—its institutions, its values, its people—was one thing and that racial slavery and oppression were a different story." This error was compounded by the tendency of American historians to create a national history which emphasized the Founders' ideas rather than their reality. The result was a history which "continued to amplify the myths of automatic progress, universal freedom, and the American dream." But in our fragmented present, this "holy history" no longer works, no longer explains our society to its people. "The present challenges the past in ways that cannot be denied. History, even as national myth, must tell us who we are, how and why we are where we are, and how our destinies have been shaped." Huggins was calling for more than the inclusion of previously ignored groups; he was calling for a new structural understanding of our history. "The challenge of the paradox," he concluded, "is that there can be no white history or black history, nor can there be an integrated history that does not begin to comprehend that slavery and freedom, white and black, are joined at the hip."[11] Extending Huggins's insight to workers, immigrants, women, and other social and ethnic groups, defines precisely the type of synthesis we need so sorely, the type of synthesis the historiography of the past few decades begins to make possible.

In his 1869 inaugural address as president of Harvard, Charles William Eliot advised his listeners that "the University must accommodate itself promptly to significant changes in the character of the people for whom it exists. The institutions of higher education in any nation are always a faithful mirror in which are sharply reflected the national history and character. In this mobile nation the action and reaction between the University and society at large are more sensitive and rapid than in stiffer communities."[12]

The course recommended by Eliot and Huggins is not an easy one. It denies us the comfort of some inexorable "truths" we have grown used to and drawn much comfort from; it replaces some certainties with paradoxes and relativities. In his presidential address to the American Historical Association in 1961, Samuel Flagg Bemis worried about precisely this trend among his fellow scholars, and asked: "Have not our social studies been tending overmuch to self-study—to what is the matter with us. . . . Too much self-study, too much self-criticism is weakening to a people as it is to an individual. There is such a thing as a national neurosis."[13]

I would argue, on the contrary, that a people's culture is safe only insofar as it continues to ceaselessly examine and understand itself. To maintain its health, Alfred North Whitehead once observed, a society must take care to prevent its codes, its rules, its canons—its entire symbolic system—from becoming fixed and hard: "All such rules and canons," Whitehead insisted, "require revision in the light of reason. . . . Those societies which cannot combine reverence to their symbols with freedom of revision, must ultimately decay either from anarchy, or from the slow atrophy of a life stifled by useless shadows."[14]

I agree with what is implicit in Eliot and Whitehead and explicit in Huggins: To teach a history that excludes large areas of American culture and ignores the experiences of significant segments of the American people is to teach a history that fails to touch us, that fails to explain America to us or to anyone else.

Epilogue

"Men make their own history," Karl Marx wrote in 1852, just a decade before Abraham Lincoln cautioned Congress about the impossibility of escaping history, "but they do not make it just as they please; they do not make it under circumstances chosen by themselves, but under circumstances directly encountered, given and transmitted from the past."[1]

We would do well to bear this truth in mind. The historical pattern of American higher education, as this book has demonstrated, has been toward increasing openness, greater inclusiveness, expanded choice, the study of the modern as well as the ancient, a concentration on American, African, and Asian as well as European culture. These have not been inventions of our own time; they have not resulted from the plots of New Left activists, the chauvinism of Afrocentrists, the philistinism of unsophisticated, gullible students, or the Machiavellianism of crafty faculty. This pattern has been the result of fundamental changes in the nature and composition of our society and has emanated from continuous encounters with those who have held a more fixed, Eurocentric, past-oriented, hierarchical conception of education. The patterns of education discussed in these pages have not developed quickly or easily, and the struggle out of which they came is not concluded. Our object should be not to end that struggle, from which much that is positive and lasting has come, but to comprehend its nature and its meaning.

Those who oppose current developments in higher education have been more successful outside than inside the universities. They have not been able to halt the continued evolution of a more eclectic, open, culturally diverse, and relevant curriculum through the persuasiveness of their case and their scholarship, but they have been exceedingly skillful in casting aspersions on and perverting the meaning of those developments. They have branded as ethnic chauvinism a multiculturalism that has finally begun to approach and explore the complexity and diversity of the United States. They have trotted out all of the disparaging adjectives older generations too frequently enjoy attaching to the young and applied them to the most diverse mixture of young people ever to constitute the student bodies of our universities whose fascinating blend of cultures makes them extraordinarily challenging and stimulating to teach. They have applied the term "political correctness" to the expanding study of the roles played by a wide variety of Americans in shaping our culture and our society. They have employed the same term to denigrate the most heartening growth of sensitivity to and awareness of human differences and vulnerabilities our universities and indeed our nation have ever experienced.

The question is not why such critics exist; they have always existed and doubtless always will. The conundrum is why in our own time have they found such resonance in American society? Why have their versions of what is taking place within higher education found such a positive reception to the point where terms like "political correctness" are treated as facts and become excuses for thought?

We might search for the answer in an intriguing shift that has taken place in the past hundred years. At the end of the nineteenth century there was a leaning toward belief in utopian visions with

the popularity of such books as Edward Bellamy's *Looking Backward,* in which Americans created a just and peaceful society by
the year 2000. At the close of the twentieth century we find the
opposite phenomenon: the gravitation toward what has been
called the "dystopian" vision of a calamitous future. We have seen
this tendency throughout this book in which the direst predictions of the death of literature, the collapse of learning, the end of
culture, the destruction of the American Republic by unassimil-
able immigrants have won adherents. Perhaps the most notable
recent example is Richard Herrnstein's and Charles Murray's
best-selling *The Bell Curve* (1994) which portrays a future dominated by what they call the "custodial state" characterized by the
division of the United States into two nations, one featuring a
"cognitive elite" of those with high IQs who will live in strongly
guarded enclaves to protect them from a low-IQ underclass inca-
pable of improvement or adjustment to the modern technological
world and forced to live in a "high-tech and more lavish version of
the Indian reservation." It is a bleak picture made even grimmer
by their prediction that "once it is accepted that a significant part
of the population must be made permanent wards of the state,"
the United States will no longer be able to preserve "its heritage
of individualism, equal rights before the law, free people running
their own lives."[2]

The faith in the future, in progress, so characteristic of nineteenth-century Americans is hardly representative of their late-
twentieth-century descendants. There are many reasons for this
shift, but perhaps one of the most potent is the sense of displace-
ment, the growing notion that we as a people are no longer what
the Puritan settlers termed a "city on a hill," no longer the destined inheritors of a preordained future. We have had more than
a few problems accepting the fact that our world was not the center of the universe nor our species necessarily at the center of
our world. It has been equally trying to accept the same news for
our nation or for the groups within the nation that saw themselves
as inherently and permanently central. "When we discover that

there are several cultures instead of just one," Paul Ricoeur has observed, " . . . when we acknowledge the end of a sort of cultural monopoly, be it illusory or real, we are threatened. . . . Suddenly it becomes possible that there are just *others*, that we ourselves are an 'other' among others."[3]

From the scientific revelations of Darwin to the current scholarship of historians and other humanists and social scientists, we have had difficulty—at times grave difficulty—adjusting to this truth. Some of us have turned on the universities in an effort to punish the messengers and have discovered the easiest and perhaps most effective way to achieve this, and at the same time preserve the comforting mythos of the past, was to distort their messages. But distortion exacts a fearful price: it makes it impossible to discover the nature and meaning of our history and our developing culture; impossible to comprehend that literature and art have not been the monopolies of certain groups and cultures in the past, but have been dynamic and living entities that Americans of all sorts have been capable of contributing to; impossible to contemplate seriously the proposition that the genius of our nation has not been to preserve and disseminate a specific culture, be it "Anglo" or "Teutonic" or "Western," but to demonstrate the possibilities of creating a truly interethnic and interracial culture which is more than a reproduction of any of its specific parts and which owes its essence to its diversity. The "exciting destiny" of the United States, observes the contemporary novelist Ishmael Reed, echoing such of his nineteenth-century predecessors as Emerson, Melville, and Whitman, stems from the fact that "the United States is unique in the world: The world is here."[4]

To create curricula, canons, and histories upon the foundation of this truth is not to subvert but to explore and build upon and celebrate what has been at the core of our history and our culture. Indeed, this very scholarship attests to the fact that what Jürgen Habermas has called the "exhaustion of utopian energies" is far from complete.[5] Those who have helped to create the new historical and scholarly standards and practices retain a great deal of faith in future possibilities. They remain convinced that widespread comprehension of the nature and intricacies of American history and identity can help to release the American population from historical myths that have prevented us from achieving self-understanding, that have separated us, and have helped to create contemporary cultural tensions and fears. An understanding of our past, our complexity, our diversity, and our cultural distinctiveness can free us to face our problems and embrace the possibilities our history, our development, our culture have given us.

We really have no other viable choice. We can no more escape history than the Americans of Lincoln's time could, and we are no less in need of his advice to "disenthrall ourselves" from "the dogmas of the quiet past." To achieve this we need not a new history but a more profound and indeed more complex understanding of our old history. This need presses down upon us relentlessly, and we will ultimately be judged by how well we meet it, by how able we are to keep our understanding of the American past—and present—open, dynamic, and responsive, free of the weight of fixed symbols and rigid canons.

Notes

Prologue

1. "STOP THAT MONUMENT," *National Review* 18 (September 18, 1981): 1064; *New York Times,* May 7, 1981, A20; October 24, 1981, A23; November 11, 1981, A30; March 27, 1981, A1, A11.

2. *New York Times,* November 10, 1982, A16; November 11, 1982, A1, A28, B15; November 13, 1982, A9; May 28, 1983, A5.

3. Marita Sturken, "The Wall, the Screen, and the Image: The Vietnam Veterans Memorial," *Representations* 35 (Summer 1991): 118–42; Charles Harbutt, "The Things They Leave Behind," *New York Times Magazine,* November 12, 1995, 83–85; Charles L. Griswold, "The Vietnam Veterans Memorial and the Washington Mall: Philosophical Thoughts on Political Iconography," *Critical Inquiry* 12 (Summer 1986): 688–719.

4. Abraham Lincoln, Annual Message to Congress, December 1, 1862, in *Abraham Lincoln: Speeches and Writings, 1859–1865* (New York: Library of America, 1989), 415.

5. Ibid.

6. William James, "What Pragmatism Means," in *William James: Writings, 1902–1910* (New York: Library of America, 1987), 521.

7. U.S. Department of Commerce, *Statistical Abstract of the United*

States, 1992 (Washington, D.C.: U.S. Government Printing Office, 1992), tables 258, 278; U.S. Department of Education, *Digest of Education Statistics, 1991* (Washington, D.C.: U.S. Government Printing Office, 1991), table 195; U.S. Department of Commerce, *Historical Statistics of the United States: Colonial Times to 1970* (Washington, D.C.: U.S. Government Printing Office, 1975), table series H 751–65; U.S. Department of Education, *Digest of Education Statistics, 1992* (Washington, D.C.: U.S. Government Printing Office, 1992), tables 212, 214.

8. Statistics concerning the University of California at Berkeley were supplied by the university's Office of Student Research. National population figures come from U.S. Department of Commerce, *Statistical Abstract of the United States, 1994* (Washington, D.C.: U.S. Government Printing Office, 1994), table 18.

Chapter 1

1. Allan Bloom, *The Closing of the American Mind: How Higher Education Has Failed Democracy and Impoverished the Souls of Today's Students* (New York: Simon and Schuster, 1987); Charles J. Sykes, *Profscam: Professors and the Demise of Higher Education* (New York: Kampmann and Co., 1988); Peter Shaw, *The War Against the Intellect: Episodes in the Decline of Discourse* (Iowa City: University of Iowa Press, 1989); Roger Kimball, *Tenured Radicals: How Politics Has Corrupted Our Higher Education* (New York: Harper and Row, 1990); Page Smith, *Killing the Spirit: Higher Education in America* (New York: Viking, 1990); Charles J. Sykes, *The Hollow Men: Politics and Corruption in Higher Education* (Washington, D.C.: Regnery Gateway, 1990); Dinesh D'Souza, *Illiberal Education: The Politics of Race and Sex on Campus* (New York: Free Press, 1991); William J. Bennett, *The De-Valuing of America: The Fight for Our Culture and Our Children* (New York: Summit Books, 1992); Martin Anderson, *Impostors in the Temple: American Intellectuals Are Destroying Our Universities and Cheating Our Students of Their Future* (New York: Simon and Schuster, 1992); Richard Bernstein, *Dictatorship of Virtue: Multiculturalism and the Battle for America's Future* (New York: Knopf, 1994).

2. Buchanan's statement is in the *San Francisco Chronicle*, August 19, 1992; Kimball, *Tenured Radicals*, 206; the ad for Thomas Aquinas Col-

lege is in *National Review,* February 20, 1995, 23; George F. Will, "Curdled Politics on Campus," *Newsweek,* May 6, 1991, 72; George F. Will, "Literary Politics," *Newsweek,* April 22, 1991, 72; Berger's remarks are in *Partisan Review 58* (1991): 317.

3. Kramer is quoted in James Atlas, *Battle of the Books: The Curriculum Debate in America* (New York: Norton, 1990), 70; Bennett, *The Devaluing of America,* 28, 33.

4. Will, "Literary Politics," 72; Gertrude Himmelfarb, *The New History and the Old* (Cambridge: Harvard University Press, 1987), 26, 14–18.

5. Bloom, *The Closing of the American Mind,* 314–15, 321. For the book's sales, see "Best Sellers From 1987's Book Crop," *New York Times,* January 6, 1988. The meetings of the NAS are reported in *New York Times,* November 15, 1988, A22; and *Chronicle of Higher Education,* November 23, 1988, A1, A11, and June 20, 1990, A15–16.

6. Bernstein, *Dictatorship of Virtue,* 3–5, 8, 48, 346; Robert Hughes, *Culture of Complaint: The Fraying of America* (New York: Oxford University Press, 1993), 24, 56–57; Smith, *Killing the Spirit,* 9, 122; Sykes, *Hollow Men,* 60; Sykes, *Profscam,* 8, 264; D'Souza, *Illiberal Education,* 228.

7. John Taylor, "Are You Politically Correct?" *New York Magazine,* January 21, 1991, 32–40; Gary Kamiya, "Civilization & Its Discontents," *San Francisco Examiner Magazine,* January 22, 1995, cover and 14–27.

8. Robert Brustein, "Dumbocracy in America," *Partisan Review 60* (1993): 527; John Patrick Diggins, *The Rise and Fall of the American Left* (New York: Norton, 1992), 298 and chap. 7; George Roche, *The Fall of the Ivory Tower: Government Funding, Corruption, and the Bankrupting of American Higher Education* (Washington, D.C.: Regnery Gateway, 1994), 3–4; Wilcomb E. Washburn, *The "Treason of the Intellectuals," 1989* (Young America's Foundation, n.d.), 2–3; Kimball, *Tenured Radicals,* xiv.

9. Bloom, *The Closing of the American Mind,* 101, 65; Smith, *Killing the Spirit,* 285–92; Sykes, *Hollow Men,* 37–39.

10. Bernstein, *Dictatorship of Virtue,* 48–50; Atlas, *Battle of the Books,* 72–73. For examples of how the Jane Austen paper is treated, see Kimball, *Tenured Radicals,* 192, 201; John Taylor, "Are You Politically Correct?" *New York Magazine,* January 21, 1991, 36.

11. Charles Krauthammer, "An Insidious Rejuvenation of the Old Left," *Los Angeles Times,* December 24, 1990; Kimball, *Tenured Radicals,* xi–xviii.

12. Bloom, *The Closing of the American Mind,* 381, 329; Anderson, *Impostors in the Temple,* 44.

13. Gertrude Himmelfarb, in *Partisan Review* 58 (1991): 362; Atlas, *Battle of the Books,* 87–88, 48–51; Kimball, *Tenured Radicals,* 204.

14. Bloom, *The Closing of the American Mind,* 135–37.

15. Ibid., 34, 65–66, 107–8, 68–81, 51.

16. For Matthew Arnold's influential and much quoted views, see his *Culture and Anarchy* (London: Smith, Elder and Co., 1875), 44, 47; John Searle, "The Storm Over the University," in Paul Berman, ed., *Debating P.C.: The Controversy Over Political Correctness on College Campuses* (New York: Laurel, 1992), 88.

17. Atlas, *Battle of the Books,* 136, 43; Clark is quoted in Samuel Eliot Morison, *Three Centuries of Harvard, 1636–1936* (Cambridge: Harvard University Press, 1936), 260; Henry Adams, *The Education of Henry Adams* (1918; New York: Modern Library edition, 1931), 55, 59–60.

18. James Atlas, in *Partisan Review* 58 (1991): 262, 264; Lawrence Auster, "America Is in Danger: Our Ability to Preserve Our Common Heritage Depends on the Continued Existence of a Majority Population that Believes in It," *Newsday,* May 12, 1991, 30.

19. Bloom, *The Closing of the American Mind,* 27, 33, 36–39, 29–30, 202.

20. Roger Kimball, "'Tenured Radicals': A Postscript," *New Criterion* 9 (January 1991): 12; Bernstein, *Dictatorship of Virtue,* 42–45; Atlas, *Battle of the Books,* 90.

21. Charles Krauthammer, "Hale Columbus, Dead White Male," *Time,* May 27, 1991; William Bennett, "Why the West?" *National Review,* May 27, 1988, 38 (italics added).

22. D'Souza, *Illiberal Education,* 33.

23. Sykes, *Profscam,* 6; Hughes, *Culture of Complaint,* 67.

24. Anderson, *Impostors in the Temple,* 85; Smith, *Killing the Spirit,* 7; Bloom, *The Closing of the American Mind,* 68–81, 65–66, 97–108, 34.

25. Kimball, *Tenured Radicals,* chap. 1; Bettina J. Huber and David Laurence, "Report on the 1984–85 Survey of the English Sample: General Education Requirements in English and the English Major," ADE

Bulletin 93 (1989): 30–43; Bettina J. Huber, "Today's Literature Classroom: Findings from the MLA's 1990 Survey of Upper-Division Courses," ADE *Bulletin* 101 (1992): 36–60; Phyllis Franklin, Bettina J. Huber, and David Laurence, "Continuity and Change in the Study of Literature," *Change* (January/February 1992): 42–48.

26. Diggins, *The Rise and Fall of the American Left*, 291, 298; Lynn V. Cheney, *Telling the Truth: A Report on the State of the Humanities in Higher Education* (Washington, D.C.: National Endowment for the Humanities, 1992), 28; Jerry Z. Muller, "Challenging Political Correctness: A 'Paranoid Hysteric' Replies to Joan Scott," *Perspectives: American Historical Association Newsletter* 31 (May/June 1993): 13–15.

27. Shaw, *The War Against the Intellect*, xiii.

28. Gertrude Himmelfarb, "Some Reflections on the New History," *American Historical Review* 94 (June 1989): 668.

29. Cheney, *Telling the Truth*, 14.

30. Himmelfarb, in *Partisan Review* 58 (1991): 362.

31. Bloom, *The Closing of the American Mind*, 321.

32. Sykes, *Hollow Men*, 17.

33. Sir Lewis Namier, "History," in Fritz Stern, ed., *The Varieties of History From Voltaire to the Present* (New York: World Publishing, 1956), 375; Raoul V. Mowatt, "What Revolution at Stanford?" in Patricia Aufderheide, ed., *Beyond PC: Toward a Politics of Understanding* (Saint Paul: Graywolf Press, 1992), 131–32.

34. Richard Hofstadter, "The Paranoid Style in American Politics," in Hofstadter, *The Paranoid Style in American Politics and Other Essays* (New York: Knopf, 1965), 3–40.

35. Lewis Carroll, *Alice's Adventures in Wonderland* in Martin Gardner, ed., *The Annotated Alice* (New York: Meridian Books, 1973), 138.

Chapter 2

1. George P. Schmidt, *The Liberal Arts College: A Chapter in American Cultural History* (New Brunswick: Rutgers University Press, 1957), 45, 55–56.

2. The Yale Report was published in slightly abbreviated form as "Original Papers in Relation to a Course of Liberal Education," in *American Journal of Science and Arts* 15 (January 1829): 297–351. The quotes in the text are from pp. 300, 330. Italics in the original.

3. Jacob Van Vechten, *Memoirs of John M. Mason with Portions of His Correspondence* (New York: R. Carter and Bros., 1856), 239; "Original Papers," 332, 345, 346, 349. The *Western Review* is quoted in R. Freeman Butts, *The College Charts Its Course: Historical Conceptions and Current Proposals* (New York: McGraw-Hill, 1939), 117.

4. John Maclean, "Inaugural Address," reprinted in John Maclean, *History of the College of New Jersey: From Its Origin in 1746 to the Commencement of 1854*, 2 vols. (Philadelphia: J. B. Lippincott Co., 1877), vol. 2, 421; *Proceedings Connected With the Semi-Centennial Commemoration of the Professorship of Rev. Charles Hodge, D.D., LL.D. in the Theological Seminary at Princeton, N.J., April 24, 1872*, 52; Lyman Beecher, *Plea for Colleges*, 2d ed. (Cincinnati: Truman and Smith, 1836), 19–20.

5. Frederick Rudolph, *Curriculum: A History of the American Undergraduate Course of Study Since 1636* (San Francisco: Jossey-Bass, 1977), 64; George Paul Schmidt, "Colleges in Ferment," *American Historical Review* 59 (October 1953): 24; Schmidt, *The Liberal Arts College*, 66. Precisely the same situation prevailed at Princeton University. See Thomas Jefferson Wertenbaker, *Princeton, 1746–1896* (Princeton: Princeton University Press, 1946), 235.

6. Frederick Rudolph, *The American College and University* (1962; Athens: University of Georgia Press, 1990), 232; the Yale student is quoted in Schmidt, *The Liberal Arts College*, 173; Fred Lewis Pattee, *Penn State Yankee: The Autobiography of Fred Lewis Pattee* (State College, Penn.: Pennsylvania State College Press, 1953), 152.

7. Schmidt, *The Liberal Arts College*, 59; Willis Rudy, *The Evolving Liberal Arts Curriculum: A Historical Review of Basic Themes* (New York: Bureau of Publications, Teachers College, Columbia University, 1960), 3; William Summerscales, *Affirmation and Dissent: Columbia's Response to the Crisis of World War I* (New York: Teachers College Press, 1970), 120–21; Lionel Trilling, "The Van Amringe and Keppel Eras," in *A History of Columbia College on Morningside* (New York: Columbia University Press, 1954), 36; Charles William Eliot, "The Case Against Compulsory Latin," *Atlantic Monthly* 119 (March 1917): 352–53.

8. Van Hise is quoted in Butts, *The College Charts Its Course*, 227–28; Charles William Eliot, "What Is a Liberal Education?" in Eliot, *Educational Reform: Essays and Addresses* (New York: Century Co., 1898),

104–5. Eliot originally delivered this as a lecture at Johns Hopkins University, February 22, 1884, and published it in *Century*, June 1884.

9. The situation of history at Harvard and McCosh's reply are in Samuel Eliot Morison, *Three Centuries of Harvard, 1636–1936* (Cambridge: Harvard University Press, 1936), 347–49. Eliot, "The Case Against Compulsory Latin," 355.

10. Francis Wayland, *Thoughts on the Present Collegiate System in the United States* (Boston: Gould, Kendall and Lincoln, 1842), 16–17, 46–48, 154–56, and passim; Francis Wayland, *Report to the Corporation of Brown University on Changes in the System of Collegiate Education* (1850), 454–55, and passim.

11. Charles William Eliot, "The New Education," *Atlantic Monthly* 23 (February and March 1869): 203–20, 358–67; the quote is on 359. The Eliot-McCosh debate was sponsored by the Nineteenth Century Club and held at the home of Courtlandt Palmer in New York City. Eliot's remarks were published in Charles William Eliot, "Liberty in Education," in Eliot, *Educational Reform*, 125–48.

12. *American Universities—What They Should Be. Inaugural Address Delivered by President James McCosh at the College of New Jersey, Princeton, October 27, 1868* (San Francisco: Turnbull and Smith, 1869), 18–19; italics in original. James McCosh, *The New Departure in College Education: Being a Reply to President Eliot's Defence of it in New York Feb. 24, 1885* (New York: C. Scribner's Sons, 1885).

13. Butts, *The College Charts its Course*, 237; Noah Porter, *The American Colleges and the American Public* (1870; New York: Arno Press, 1969), 48–49, 51, 58–59, and passim.

14. Andrew F. West, "Must the Classics Go?" *North American Review* 138 (February 1884): 151–62; Caleb Mills, *New Departures in Collegiate Control and Culture* (New York: A. S. Barnes and Co., 1880), 25–32.

15. Lowell's inaugural address is reprinted in A. Lawrence Lowell, *At War with Academic Traditions in America* (Cambridge: Harvard University Press, 1934), 32–45. For more on Lowell's thought concerning electives and concentration and distribution, see the following essays, addresses, and reports, in this volume: "The Choice of Electives" (1887), "Competition in College" (1909), "Culture" (1915), "Changes in the Elective System" (1908–9).

16. Charles Mills Gayley, *Idols of Education* (1910; Garden City: Doubleday, 1916), 96–97; Morison, *Three Centuries of Harvard, 1636–1936,* 389–90.

17. Robert Maynard Hutchins, *The Higher Learning in America* (New Haven: Yale University Press, 1936), passim. For a comprehensive reply to Hutchins, see Harry D. Gideonse, *The Higher Learning in a Democracy: A Reply to President Hutchins' Critique of the American University* (New York: Farrar and Rinehart, 1937).

18. J. Winfree Smith, *A Search for the Liberal College: The Beginning of the St. John's Program* (Annapolis: St. John's College Press, 1983), 2; Allan Bloom, *The Closing of the American Mind* (New York: Simon and Schuster, 1987), 344.

19. Mark Van Doren, *Liberal Education* (New York: Henry Holt and Co., 1943), 110 ff., 144 ff., 81.

20. Scott Buchanan, *Poetry and Mathematics* (Philadelphia: Keystone Books, 1962), 27–28; Mortimer J. Adler, *Philosopher at Large: An Intellectual Autobiography* (New York: Macmillan, 1977), 175–76.

21. Smith, *A Search for the Liberal College,* chaps. 1–4. The Lippmann quote is on p. 39.

22. Hutchins's statement on metaphysics is in his *The Higher Learning in America,* 105. For the origins and development of the Great Books course at Columbia, see John Erskine's two autobiographies, *The Memory of Certain Persons* (Philadelphia: J. B. Lippincott Co., 1947), 342–45; and *My Life as a Teacher* (Philadelphia: J. B. Lippincott Co., 1948), chap. 12. The Erskine quote is from *Memory,* 343. For the Great Books curriculum at Chicago see James Sloan Allen, *The Romance of Commerce and Culture: Capitalism, Modernism, and the Chicago-Aspen Crusade for Cultural Reform* (Chicago: University of Chicago Press, 1983), chap. 3. For an early and extremely popular Great Books course which Charles Mills Gayley established at Berkeley in 1901, see Henry F. May, *Three Faces of Berkeley: Competing Ideologies in the Wheeler Era, 1899–1901* (Berkeley: Center for Studies in Higher Education, 1993), 35.

23. Hutchins's and Adler's efforts to spread Great Books to the public are discussed in Allen, *The Romance of Commerce and Culture,* 99–106, and Robert Hutchins, *The Great Conversation* (Chicago: Encyclopedia Britannica, 1952). The quote from Hutchins is on p. 3; see also

chap. 4: "The Disappearance of Liberal Education." Bloom's views are in *The Closing of the American Mind*, 344.

24. The "vicious specialization" term is from Hutchins, *The Great Conversation*, xxiv; "chaos" and "anarchic individualism" are from Adler below, pp. 98, 103. Adler's address "God and the Professors," was delivered at the Conference on Science, Philosophy, and Religion on September 10, 1940, and printed in *Vital Speeches of the Day* 7 (December 1, 1940): 98–103; Adler's references to students were made in his article, "This Pre-War Generation," *Harper's Magazine*, 181 (October 1940): 524–34.

25. Adler, "God and the Professors," *Vital Speeches of the Day*, 7 (December 1, 1940), 99; Adler, "This Pre-War Generation," *Harper's Magazine*, 181 (October 1940), 533.

Chapter 3

1. Daniel Boorstin, *America and the Image of Europe: Reflections on American Thought* (New York: Meridian Books, 1960), 19–20, 38. For the effects of World War I upon interest in European history in the United States, see Leonard Krieger, "European History in America," in John Higham, Leonard Krieger, and Felix Gilbert, *History: The Development of Historical Studies in the United States* (Englewood Cliffs: Prentice-Hall, 1965), especially 268–87. Everett S. Brown, "Freshman History at the University of California," *History Teacher's Magazine* 7 (October 1916): 268–69; Irwin Edman, *Philosopher's Holiday* (New York: Viking, 1938), 131.

2. Carol S. Gruber, *Mars and Minerva: World War I and the Uses of the Higher Learning in America* (Baton Rouge: Louisiana State University Press, 1975), 214–19, 238–42; Albert Kerr Heckel, "The War Aims Course in the Colleges," *Historical Outlook* 10 (January 1919): 20–22.

3. Gruber, *Mars and Minerva*, 243–44. For a detailed discussion of the content and development of these courses, see Justus Buchler, "Reconstruction in the Liberal Arts," in *A History of Columbia College on Morningside* (New York: Columbia University Press, 1954), 48–135. See also Harry J. Carman, "Reminiscences of Thirty Years," *Journal of Higher Education* 22 (March 1951): 115–22; H. E. Hawkes, "A College Course on Peace Issues," *Educational Review* 58 (June-December 1919): 143–50.

4. Schurman is quoted in William Summerscales, *Affirmation and Dissent: Columbia's Response to the Crisis of World War I* (New York: Teachers College Press, 1970), 138.

5. Salmon's views are part of the report by The Committee of Seven, *The Study of History in Schools: Report to the American Historical Association* (1899; New York: Macmillan, 1912), 162–63.

6. Nicholas Murray Butler, *The Rise of a University: From the Annual Reports, 1902–1935, of Nicholas Murray Butler, President of Columbia University*, Edward C. Elliott, ed., 2 vols. (New York: Columbia University Press, 1937), vol. 2, 220–27; Carolyn C. Lougee, comments in the *American Historical Review* 87 (June 1982): 726–29.

7. Lionel Trilling, "The Van Amringe and Keppel Eras," in *A History of Columbia College on Morningside*, 14–47; Herbert Hawkes is quoted by Trilling on p. 37; Frederick Paul Keppel, *Columbia* (New York: Oxford University Press, 1914), 179–81.

8. For an excellent discussion of the evolution of the Western Civ course, see Gilbert Allardyce, "The Rise and Fall of the Western Civilization Course," *American Historical Review* 87 (June 1982): 695–725. Justus Buchler, "Reconstruction in the Liberal Arts," in *A History of Columbia College on Morningside*, 101; James Harvey Robinson, *The Ordeal of Civilization* (New York: Harper and Bros., 1926), 4, 727.

9. Sydney Smith, "Review of Adam Seybert, Statistical Annals of the United States of America," *Edinburgh Review* 33 (1820): 79–80; Henry James, *Hawthorne* (1879; Ithaca: Cornell University Press, 1967), 34–35.

10. John Adams to Thomas Jefferson, reprinted in Richard Hofstadter and Wilson Smith, eds., *American Higher Education: A Documentary History*, 2 vols. (Chicago: University of Chicago Press, 1961), vol. 1, 232; Thomas Jefferson, *Notes on the State of Virginia* (Chapel Hill: University of North Carolina Press, 1955), 84–85; Jefferson's "ocean of fire" statement and the comments by Buchanan and Crawford are in Roy L. Garis, *Immigration Restriction: A Study of the Opposition to and Regulation of Immigration into the United States* (New York: Macmillan, 1927), 26, 34; John Quincy Adams to Baron von Furstenwaerther, printed in *Nile's Weekly Register* 18 (April 29, 1820): 127–28; Henry David Thoreau, *Walking* (Cambridge: Riverside Press, 1914), 86–87; Walt Whitman, *Democratic Vistas* (1871), in *Walt Whitman: Complete Poetry*

and Collected Prose (New York: Library of America, 1982), 961; Walt Whitman, *Leaves of Grass* (1855), ibid., 87.

11. Werner Sollors, *Beyond Ethnicity: Consent and Descent in American Culture* (New York: Oxford University Press, 1986), 7; Frederick Jackson Turner, "The Significance of the Frontier in American History," Harold P. Simonson, ed. (New York: Ungar, 1990), 44.

12. Carlton J. H. Hayes, *A Political and Cultural History of Modern Europe*, 2 vols. (New York: Macmillan, 1932), vol. 1, vii. Wriston is quoted in Russell Thomas, *The Search for a Common Learning: General Education, 1800–1960* (New York: McGraw-Hill, 1962), 88–89.

13. See Gilbert Allardyce, "The Rise and Fall of the Western Civilization Course," *American Historical Review* 87 (June 1982): 716–18.

14. This AHA session, "Beyond Western Civilization: Rebuilding the Survey," was published in its entirety, along with additional comments in *History Teacher* 10 (August 1977): 509–48. The quote from Professor Cheyette is on p. 537.

15. See *General Education in a Free Society: Report of the Harvard Committee* (Cambridge: Harvard University Press, 1945), 205–7, 213–17. For the debate on the proposals of this report, see David Owen, "Harvard General Education in Social Science," *Journal of General Education* 5 (October 1950): 17–30. See also Daniel Bell, *The Reforming of General Education* (New York: Columbia University Press, 1966), 38–50.

16. *The Study of Education at Stanford*, 10 vols. (Stanford: Stanford University Press, 1968), vol. 1, 13–15; vol. 2, 5–11. Scaver's views are expressed in his letter of September 10, 1968, in vol. 2, app. 4.

17. Carnegie Commission on Higher Education, *Reform on Campus: Changing Students, Changing Academic Programs* (New York: McGraw–Hill, 1972), 42–47.

18. Allardyce, "The Rise and Fall of the Western Civilization Course," 716, 723; *Introduction to Contemporary Civilization in the West: A Source Book Prepared by the Contemporary Civilization Staff of Columbia College, Columbia University*, 2 vols. (New York: Columbia University Press, 1946), vol. 1, v; Lionel Trilling, "The Uncertain Future of the Humanistic Educational Ideal," *American Scholar* 44 (Winter 1974–75): 52–67.

19. *Newsweek*, February 1, 1988, 46; *San Francisco Chronicle*, April 1, 1988, A7.

20. Bennett's views are from the *San Francisco Chronicle,* February 5, 1988, April 1, 1988, and the *Chronicle of Higher Education,* February 10, 1988, A19, A27; February 17, 1988, A16. William Bennett, "Why the West?" *National Review,* May 27, 1988, 37–39, is an adaptation of his speech at Stanford University.

21. Unless otherwise noted, my discussion of the Stanford debate is derived from Herbert Lindenberger, "The Western Culture Debate at Stanford University," *Comparative Criticism: An Annual Journal* 2 (Fall 1989): 225–34; Mary Louise Pratt, "Humanities for the Future: Reflections on the Western Culture Debate at Stanford," in Darryl J. Gless and Barbara Herrnstein Smith, eds., *The Politics of Liberal Education* (Durham: Duke University Press, 1992), 13–31; Daniel Gordon, "Inside the Stanford Mind," *Perspectives: American Historical Association Newsletter,* 30 (April 1992): 1, 4, 7–8; and especially from the superb collection of sources, "The Discussion About Proposals to Change the Western Culture Program at Stanford University," *Minerva, Review of Science, Learning and Policy* 27 (Summer-Autumn 1989): 223–411, which includes many substantial excerpts from the debate in the Faculty Senate.

22. Katz is quoted in *Newsweek,* February 1, 1988, 46.

23. King's remarks about Great Books and his expectations are quoted in *Newsweek,* February 1, 1988, 46; his speech to the Faculty Senate is in "The Discussion About Proposals to Change the Western Culture Program," 224–25, 299–303.

24. Judith C. Brown, letter to the editor, *Perspectives: American Historical Association Newsletter* 30 (November 1992): 11; Raoul V. Mowatt, "What Revolution at Stanford?" in Patricia Aufderheide, ed., *Beyond PC: Toward a Politics of Understanding* (Saint Paul: Graywolf Press, 1992), 129.

25. For Bennett's Stanford speech, see "The Discussion About Proposals to Change the Western Culture Program," 394–400; Dinesh D'Souza, *Illiberal Education: The Politics of Race and Sex on Campus* (New York: Free Press, 1991), 92; James Atlas, *Battle of the Books* (New York: Norton, 1990), 73.

26. For the reforms proposed by Ticknor and Wayland, see George Ticknor, *Remarks on Changes Lately Proposed or Adopted in Harvard*

University (Boston: Cummings, Hilliard and Co., 1825) and Francis Wayland, *Thoughts on the Present Collegiate System in the United States* (Boston: Gould, Kendall and Lincoln, 1842), and *Report to the Corporation of Brown University on Changes in the System of Collegiate Education* (1850). Barnard is quoted in George P. Schmidt, *The Liberal Arts College* (New Brunswick: Rutgers University Press, 1957), 165.

Chapter 4

1. Alvin Kernan, *The Death of Literature* (New Haven: Yale University Press, 1990), 2.

2. Ibid., 2, 5, 212.

3. Liz McMillen, "Literature's Jeremiah Leaps Into the Fray," *Chronicle of Higher Education,* September 7, 1994, A11; Harold Bloom, *The Western Canon: The Books and School of the Ages* (New York: Harcourt Brace, 1994), chaps. 1, 23.

4. John Maclean, "Inaugural Address," reprinted in John Maclean, *History of the College of New Jersey: From Its Origin in 1746 to the Commencement of 1854,* 2 vols. (Philadelphia: J. B. Lippincott Co., 1877), vol. 2, 421. The Evert Topping incident is related in Thomas Jefferson Wertenbaker, *Princeton, 1746–1896* (Princeton: Princeton University Press, 1946), 234–35.

5. Henry E. Shepherd, "English Philology and English Literature in American Universities," *Sewanee Review* 1 (November 1892): 158. For many other examples, see Gerald Graff, *Professing Literature: An Institutional History* (Chicago: University of Chicago Press, 1987), chap. 2.

6. The Princeton-Rutgers library hours are in George P. Schmidt, *Princeton and Rutgers: The Two Colonial Colleges of New Jersey* (Princeton: Van Nostrand, 1964), 35–37. The Eliot-Winsor anecdote is in Edward P. Alexander, *Museum Masters* (Nashville: American Association for State and Local History, 1983), 382.

7. The Princeton undergraduate's views are in Wertenbaker, *Princeton, 1746–1896,* 235–36. Thomas Lounsbury is quoted in Fred Lewis Pattee, "American Literature in the College Curriculum," *Educational Review* 67 (May 1924): 266. Students in the Harvard English course read Vernon's *Anglo-Saxon Guide,* Morris's *Specimens of Early English,* Chaucer's "Prologue" and "Knight's Tale," Thorpe's *Analecta Anglo-*

Saxonica, and Matzner's *Alt-Englische Sprachproben.* See Henry James, *Charles W. Eliot: President of Harvard University, 1869–1909,* 2 vols. (Boston: Houghton Mifflin, 1930), vol. 1, 211. Katharine Lee Bates's thoughts are in her article, "English at Wellesley College," in *English in American Universities,* William Morton Payne, ed., (Boston: D.C. Heath, 1895), 148.

8. Child is quoted in Phyllis Franklin, "English Studies: The World of Scholarship in 1883," *Publications of the Modern Language Association* 99 (May 1984): 367; Lowell made his remarks in an 1887 address later published as, "Shakespeare's Richard III," *Atlantic Monthly* 68 (December 1891): 817–23.

9. Charles W. Eliot, "What is a Liberal Education?" in Eliot, *Educational Reform: Essays and Addresses* (New York: Century Co., 1898), 97–98. This address was originally given at Johns Hopkins University, February 22, 1884, and published in *Century,* June 1884.

10. Francis A. March, "Recollections of Language Teaching," a talk first delivered at the Modern Language Association in 1892 and reprinted in Gerald Graff and Michael Warner, eds., *The Origins of Literary Studies in America: A Documentary Anthology* (New York: Routledge, 1989), 25–26; Francis A. March, "English at Lafayette College," in Payne, *English in American Universities,* 78; Fred Lewis Pattee, *Penn State Yankee: The Autobiography of Fred Lewis Pattee* (State College: Pennsylvania State College Press, 1953), 115; Frank Norris, "The 'English' Classes of the University of California," originally published in *The Wave* (1896) and reprinted in Graff and Warner, *Origins of Literary Studies in America,* 133–35; Shepherd, "English Philology and English Literature in American Universities," 153–59.

11. Martin W. Sampson, "English at the University of Indiana," in Payne, *English in American Universities,* 96; Albert H. Tolman, "English at the University of Chicago," ibid., 86, 89–90; William Morton Payne, "Introduction," ibid., 26.

12. Francis A. March, "Recollections of Language Teaching," a talk first delivered at the Modern Language Association in 1892 and reprinted in Graff and Warner, *Origins of Literary Studies in America,* 27.

13. On the sacralization of Shakespeare, see Lawrence W. Levine, *Highbrow/Lowbrow: The Emergence of Cultural Hierarchy in America* (Cambridge: Harvard University Press, 1988), chap. 1.

14. John S. Hart, *A Manual of American Literature: A Text-Book for Schools and Colleges* (Philadelphia: Eldredge and Bro., 1873), 25; the reviewer is quoted in Fred Lewis Pattee, "Is There an American Literature?" *Dial* 21 (November 1, 1896): 243; Henry S. Pancoast, *An Introduction to American Literature* (1898; New York: Henry Holt and Co., 1900), 2, 6; Pattee, "Is There An American Literature?" 243–45. Pattee spoke of the reaction to his article in his book, *Tradition and Jazz* (New York: Century Co., 1925), 213–14, and his autobiography, *Penn State Yankee*, 168–69.

15. Harold E. Stearns, ed., *Civilization in the United States: An Enquiry by Thirty Americans* (London and New York: Harcourt Brace, 1922), vii; Howard Mumford Jones, "American Scholarship and American Literature," *American Literature* 8 (1936–37): 120; Cooper is quoted in Pattee, *Penn State Yankee*, 117–18.

16. Arthur Hobson Quinn, "American Literature as a Subject for Graduate Study," *Educational Review* 69 (June 1922): 7–15; Robert E. Spiller, *Late Harvest: Essays and Addresses in American Literature and Culture* (Westport: Greenwood Press, 1981), 188, 207; Norman Foerster, ed., *The Reinterpretation of American Literature: Some Contributions Toward the Understanding of Its Historical Development* (New York: Harcourt Brace, 1928), viii; the statistic concerning Chaucer is in Committee on the College Study of American Literature and Culture, *American Literature in the College Curriculum* (Chicago: National Council of Teachers of English, 1948), 19; the material on Matthiessen is in Kermit Vanderbilt, *American Literature and the Academy: The Roots, Growth, and Maturity of a Profession* (Philadelphia: University of Pennsylvania Press, 1986), 470.

17. Ferner Nuhn, "Teaching American Literature in American Colleges," *American Mercury* 13 (March 1928): 328; Floyd Stovall, "What Price American Literature? American Scholar and American Literature," *Sewanee Review* 49 (October-December 1941): 469–70.

18. Jones, "American Scholarship and American Literature," 115–24; George Santayana, *The Last Puritan: A Memoir in the Form of a Novel* (1935; Cambridge: MIT Press, 1994), 178.

19. Leonard Koester, "Where is the American Department?" *Journal of Higher Education* 11 (March 1940): 135–37; Nuhn, "Teaching American Literature in American Colleges," 330–31.

20. Committee on the College Study of American Literature and Culture, *American Literature in the College Curriculum*, 16, 22–25; William H. Goetzmann, "A View of American Studies," in "Some Voices In and Around American Studies," *American Quarterly* 31 (Bibliography Issue 1979): 376–77; Robert Maynard Hutchins, *The Great Conversation: The Substance of a Liberal Education* (Chicago: Encylcopedia Britannica, 1952), xix.

21. Alfred Kazin, *On Native Grounds: An Interpretation of Modern American Prose Literature* (1942; New York: Harcourt Brace Jovanovich, 1970), 485, 488, 518; Robert Spiller, "Higher Education and the War," *Journal of Higher Education* 13 (June 1942): 295–97.

22. Roosevelt is quoted in Spiller, "Higher Education and the War," 294. For some thoughts and figures concerning the effects of the war and its aftermath upon literary studies, see Vanderbilt, *American Literature and the Academy,* chap. 26; Philip Gleason, "World War II and the Development of American Studies," *American Quarterly* 36 (Bibliography Issue 1984): 343–58; Leo Marx, "Thoughts on the Origin and Character of the American Studies Movement," *American Quarterly* 31 (Bibliography Issue, 1979): 398–401; Geraldine Murphy, "Romancing the Center: Cold War Politics and Classic American Literature," *Poetics Today* 9, no. 4 (1988): 737–47; Tremaine McDowell, *American Studies* (Minneapolis: University of Minnesota Press, 1948); Committee on the College Study of American Literature and Culture, *American Literature in the College Curriculum.*

23. Spiller, *Late Harvest,* 126–27; Vanderbilt, *American Literature and the Academy,* 540; Committee on the College Study of American Literature and Culture, *American Literature in the College Curriculum,* 23.

24. Committee on the College Study of American Literature and Culture, *American Literature in the College Curriculum,* 32–33; McDowell, *American Studies,* 26; Gene Wise, "'Paradigm Dramas' in American Studies: A Cultural and Institutional History of the Movement," *American Quarterly* 31 (Bibliography Issue 1979): 317 n. 38, 309 n. 24.

25. McDowell, *American Studies,* 93; David Levin, *Exemplary Elders* (Athens: University of Georgia Press, 1990), 123–29.

26. Spiller, *Late Harvest,* 144. For the internationalization of Ameri-

can Studies, see, Sigmund Skard, *American Studies in Europe: Their History and Present Organization,* 2 vols. (Philadelphia: University of Pennsylvania Press, 1958), and Robert Walker, *American Studies Abroad* (Westport: Greenwood Press, 1975).

Chapter 5

1. Jane Tompkins, *Sensational Designs: The Cultural Work of American Fiction 1790–1860* (New York: Oxford University Press, 1985), 99–100.

2. Paul Lauter, *Canons and Contexts* (New York: Oxford University Press, 1991), 24, 35. See also Cecelia Tichi, "American Literary Studies to the Civil War," in *Redrawing the Boundaries: The Transformation of English and American Literary Studies,* Stephen Greenblatt and Giles Gunn, eds. (New York: Modern Language Association of America, 1992).

3. Tompkins, *Sensational Designs,* chap. 1. The quote is on p. 35.

4. John S. Hart, *A Manual of American Literature* (Philadelphia: Eldridge and Bro., 1873), 105 and passim; Fred Lewis Pattee, *Century Readings for a Course in American Literature* (1919; New York: Century Co., 1922).

5. Louis Untermeyer, *American Poetry From the Beginning to Whitman* (New York: Harcourt Brace, 1931); Louis Untermeyer, *Modern American Poetry, Modern British Poetry,* Combined ed. (New York: Harcourt Brace, 1936).

6. Perry Miller et al., *Major Writers of America,* 2 vols. (New York: Harcourt, Brace and World, 1962), vol. 1, xviii; Leon Edel et al., *Masters of American Literature,* 2 vols. (Boston: Houghton Mifflin, 1959). For discussions of the anthologies mentioned in this and the preceding paragraphs, see Ernece B. Kelly, ed., *Searching for America* (Urbana: National Council of Teachers of English, 1972); H. Bruce Franklin, *The Victim as Criminal and Artist: Literature from the American Prison* (New York: Oxford University Press, 1978), xiii–xxii; Lauter, *Canons and Contexts,* 22–47; Tompkins, *Sensational Designs,* chap. 7.

7. Paul Lauter et al., *The Heath Anthology of American Literature,* 2 vols. (Lexington: Heath, 1990); Donald McQuade et al., *The Harper American Literature,* 2 vols., 2d ed. (New York: Harper Collins, 1993).

8. Harold H. Kolb, Jr., "Defining the Canon," in *Redefining Ameri-*

can Literary History, A. LaVonne Brown Ruoff and Jerry W. Ward, Jr., eds. (New York: Modern Language Association of America, 1990), 35–51.

9. George Perkins Marsh, *Human Knowledge* (1847), 14, quoted in Phyllis Franklin, "English Studies: The World of Scholarship in 1883," *Publications of the Modern Language Association* 99 (May 1984): 358; Charles William Eliot, "Liberty in Education," in Eliot, *Educational Reform* (New York: Century Co., 1898), 125–48.

10. Stephen R. Graubard, "Western Civ and Its Children," *New York Times Book Review,* July 24, 1988, 27.

11. Alvin Kernan, *The Death of Literature* (New Haven: Yale University Press, 1990), Introduction.

Chapter 6

1. Alexis de Tocqueville to Ernest de Chabrol, June 9, 1831, in Tocqueville, *Selected Letters on Politics and Society,* Roger Boesche, ed. (Berkeley: University of California Press, 1985), 38.

2. Hector St. John de Crèvecoeur, "Letter III: What Is an American?" in Crèvecoeur, *Letters from an American Farmer* (1782; New York: Penguin, 1981), 66–70.

3. *The Journals and Miscellaneous Notebooks of Ralph Waldo Emerson* (Cambridge: Harvard University Press, 1971), ix, 299–300; Herman Melville, *Redburn: His First Voyage* (1849; New York: A. and C. Boni, 1924), 189–91.

4. Frederick Jackson Turner, "The Significance of the Frontier in American History," in Turner, *The Frontier in American History* (1920; New York: Henry Holt and Co., 1928), 23; Frederick Jackson Turner, "Middle Western Pioneer Democracy," ibid., 351.

5. Israel Zangwill, *The Melting Pot* (1909; New York: Macmillan, 1920).

6. Benjamin Franklin, *Observations Concerning the Increase of Mankind* (Boston: S. Kneeland, 1755), 14–15. Italics in the original.

7. Stewart G. Cole and Mildred Wiese Cole, *Minorities and the American Promise* (New York: Harper, 1954), 135–40; Abraham Reincke, "Reincke's Journal of a Visit among the Swedes of West Jersey, 1754," *Pennsylvania Magazine of History and Biography* 23 (1909): 101; David Ramsay, *History of South Carolina from Its First Settlement in 1670, to the Year 1808* (Charleston: David Longworth, 1809), vol. 1, 22–23.

8. John Quincy Adams to Baron von Furstenwaerther, published in *Niles Weekly Register* 18 (April 29, 1820): 157–58.

9. Thomas Jefferson, *Notes on the State of Virginia* (1787; Chapel Hill: University of North Carolina Press, 1955), 83–85; Benjamin Rush, "Of the Mode of Education Proper in a Republic," in *Essays, Literary, Moral and Philosophical* (1786; Schenectady: Union College Press, 1988), 5, 7–9.

10. Lewis S. Gannett, "Is America Anti-Semitic?" *Nation* (March 21, 1923): 330–31.

11. See Jonathan Schwartz, "Henry Ford's Melting Pot," in Otto Feinstein, ed., *Ethnic Groups in the City: Culture, Institutions, and Power* (Lexington: Heath Lexington Books, 1971), 191–98; Stephen Meyer, "Adapting the Immigrant to the Line: Americanization in the Ford Factory, 1914–1921," *Journal of Social History* 14 (Fall 1980): 67–82.

12. The Marquis quote is on p. 74 of Meyer, "Adapting the Immigrant to the Line"; the Ford quote is on p. 191 of Schwartz, "Henry Ford's Melting Pot."

13. Ellwood P. Cubberly, *Changing Conceptions of Education* (Boston: Houghton Mifflin, 1909), 15–16; the New York schools superintendent is quoted in Isaac Berkson, *Theories of Americanization: A Critical Study* (New York: Columbia University Press, 1920), 59; Gino Speranza, *Race or Nation: A Conflict of Divided Loyalties* (Indianapolis: Bobbs-Merrill, 1925), 157; the 1902 poster is mentioned in Cole and Cole, *Minorities and the American Promise*, 137.

14. Ramsay, *History of South Carolina from Its First Settlement in 1670, to the Year 1808*, vol. 1, 22–23; Crèvecoeur, *Letters from an American Farmer*, 69.

15. Horace M. Kallen, "Democracy *versus* the Melting Pot," *Nation* (February 18, 1915): 190–94; (February 25, 1915): 217–20. This and other relevant essays have been reprinted in Horace Kallen, *Culture and Democracy in the United States: Studies in the Group Psychology of the American Peoples* (New York: Boni and Liveright, 1924). It is in this volume that Kallen seems to have first used the term "cultural pluralism." See p. 11.

16. Randolph Bourne, "Trans-National America," *Atlantic Monthly* (July 1916): 86–97. Bourne's ideas can also be found in two collections of his essays: *War and the Intellectuals: Essays by Randolph Bourne,*

1915–1919, Carl Resek, ed. (New York: Harper and Row, 1964), and *The Radical Will: Selected Writings, 1911–1918* (New York: Urizen Books, 1977).

17. W. E. B. Du Bois, "The Conservation of the Races," in *The American Negro Academy Occasional Papers* No. 2 (1897), 5–15.

18. W. E. B. Du Bois, "Of Our Spiritual Strivings," in Du Bois, *The Souls of Black Folk* (1903; New York: Dodd Mead, 1961), 15–22.

19. Hansen originally formulated these ideas in a 1938 address, "The Problem of the Third Generation Immigrant," which was published as "The Third Generation in America," *Commentary* 14 (November 1952): 492–500. His original address has recently been reprinted in a volume of commentaries on his thesis: Peter Kivisto and Dag Blanck, eds., *American Immigrants and Their Generations: Studies and Commentaries on the Hansen Thesis after Fifty Years* (Urbana: University of Illinois Press, 1990), 191–203.

20. Milton Gordon, *Assimilation in American Life: The Role of Race, Religion, and National Origins* (New York: Oxford University Press, 1964), 157; Talcott Parsons, "Full Citizenship for the Negro American? A Sociological Problem," in Talcott Parsons and Kenneth B. Clark, eds., *The Negro American* (Boston: Houghton Mifflin, 1967), 739.

Chapter 7

1. Arthur Schlesinger, Jr., *The Disuniting of America* (New York: Norton, 1992), 15, 17, 121; Lawrence Auster, "America is in Danger," *Newsday*, May 12, 1991, 30; Peter Brimelow, *Alien Nation: Common Sense About America's Immigration Disaster* (New York: Random House, 1995), xv.

2. George F. Kennan, *Around the Cragged Hill: A Personal and Political Philosophy* (New York: Norton, 1993), chap. 7, esp. pp. 151–56.

3. Richard D. Lamm and Gary Imhoff, *The Immigration Time Bomb: The Fragmenting of America* (New York: Truman Talley Books, 1985), 119; *New York Times*, October 15, 1994.

4. Mather is quoted in Roy L. Garis, *Immigration Restriction: A Study of the Opposition to and Regulation of Immigration into the United States* (New York: Macmillan, 1927), 6, 10; Franklin is quoted in Garis, *Immigration Restriction*, 10, and in Maurice R. Davie, *World Immigra-*

tion: With Special Reference to the United States (New York: Macmillan, 1936), 36; the Pennsylvania governor and his secretary are quoted in Stewart G. Cole and Mildred Wiese Cole, *Minorities and the American Promise: The Conflict of Principle and Practice* (New York: Harper, 1954), 135.

5. Ray Allen Billington, *The Protestant Crusade 1800–1860: A Study of the Origins of American Nativism* (1938; Gloucester: Peter Smith, 1963), chap. 5. Marryat is quoted on p. 122.

6. Ibid., chap. 13. Bell is quoted on p. 326; *The Diary of George Templeton Strong*, Allan Nevins and Milton Halsey Thomas, eds., 4 vols. (1952; New York: Octagon Books, 1974), vol. 2, 320, 348; vol. 3, 335–36; Senator Davis is quoted in Garis, *Immigration Restriction*, 38.

7. The Commission on Immigration is quoted in Laura Karolina Capps, "'America for Americans!' The Call for Immigration Restriction: A Comparative Study of Two Immigration Debates," unpublished Honors Thesis (Department of History, University of California, Berkeley, 1994), 7; Josiah Strong, *Our Country: Its Possible Future and Its Present Crisis* (New York: Baker and Tylor, 1885), chaps. 4, 5, 13.

8. Henry James, *The American Scene* (1907; Bloomington: Indiana University Press, 1968), 125, 117–18, 131–34.

9. J. Appleton Morgan, "What Shall We Do With The Dago?" *Popular Science Monthly* (December 1890): 172–79; James, *The American Scene*, 132, 231.

10. Edward Alsworth Ross, *The Old World in the New: The Significance of Past and Present Immigration to the American People* (New York: Century Co., 1914), chap. 12. Italics in original. Madison Grant, *The Passing of the Great Race* (New York: C. Scribner, 1916), 80–81, 228, and passim.

11. Vernon Wharton, *The Negro in Mississippi* (New York: Harper and Row, 1965), 53–54; Joel Williamson, *After Slavery: The Negro in South Carolina During Reconstruction, 1861–1877* (Chapel Hill: University of North Carolina Press, 1965), 247.

12. Darwin is quoted in George W. Stocking, Jr., *Race, Culture, and Evolution: Essays in the History of Anthropology* (New York: Free Press, 1968), 113; for these predictions, see George M. Frederickson, *The Black Image in the White Mind: The Debate on Afro-American Character and Destiny, 1817–1914* (New York: Harper and Row, 1971), 240–42.

Chapter 8

1. Talcott Parsons, "Some Theoretical Considerations on the Nature and Trends of Change of Ethnicity," in Nathan Glazer and Daniel P. Moynihan, eds., *Ethnicity: Theory and Experience* (Cambridge: Harvard University Press, 1975), 63–64.

2. Milton M. Gordon, *Assimilation in American Life: The Role of Race, Religion, and National Origin* (New York: Oxford University Press, 1964), chap. 3 and passim; Milton M. Gordon, "Assimilation in America: Theory and Reality," *Daedalus* 90 (Spring 1961): 263–85.

3. Robert Ezra Park, "Human Migration and the Marginal Man," *American Journal of Sociology* 33 (May 1928): 881–93, reprinted in Robert Ezra Park, *Race and Culture* (Glencoe: Free Press, 1950), 345–56; See also Oscar Handlin, *The Uprooted* (Boston: Little Brown, 1951).

4. Lawrence W. Levine, *Black Culture and Black Consciousness: Afro-American Folk Thought from Slavery to Freedom* (New York: Oxford University Press, 1977), 293–96.

5. Gerard Postiglione, *Ethnicity and American Social Theory: Toward Critical Pluralism* (Lanham: University Press of America, 1983), 6–7, 203–6; Michael Novak, "Pluralism: A Humanistic Perspective," in Stephan Thernstrom, ed., *Harvard Encyclopedia of American Ethnic Groups* (Cambridge: Harvard University Press, 1980), 774–76.

6. For the work of this group see, Postiglione, *Ethnicity and American Social Theory;* Gordon, *Assimilation in American Life;* Nathan Glazer and Daniel Patrick Moynihan, *Beyond the Melting Pot: The Negroes, Puerto Ricans, Jews, Italians, and Irish of New York City* (1963; 2d ed., Cambridge: MIT Press, 1970); Francis X. Femminella, "The Immigrant and the Urban Melting Pot," in Melvin I. Urofsky, ed., *Perspectives on Urban America* (Garden City: Anchor Press, 1973), 43–65; Andrew Greeley, *Ethnicity in the United States* (New York: Wiley, 1974); Michael Novak, *The Rise of the Unmeltable Ethnics: Politics and Culture in the Seventies* (New York: Macmillan, 1972). The quotations are in Glazer and Moynihan, *Beyond the Melting Pot,* xiii–xiv, xxxiii, xcvii–xcviii, 12–16, 315. See also, Glazer and Moynihan, "Introduction," in their edited volume, *Ethnicity,* 1–26.

7. Francis X. Femminella, "The Immigrant and the Urban Melting Pot," in Urofsky, *Perspectives on Urban America,* 43–65.

8. Ulf Hannerz, "American Culture: Creolized, Creolizing," unpublished keynote address to the Nordic Association for American Studies, Uppsala, May 28, 1987. A number of these ideas are also contained in a published paper by Hannerz, "The World in Creolisation," *Africa* 57, no. 4 (1987), 546–59. For a rare, and quite different, application of the concept of creole to the early history of the United States, see Benedict Anderson, *Imagined Communities: Reflections on the Origin and Spread of Nationalism* (1983; New York: Verso, 1991), chap. 4: "Creole Pioneers."

9. Deborah Sontag, "A Romanian Poet Examines the Land of Immigrants," *New York Times,* July 11, 1993, H22.

10. Ludwig Lewisohn, *Up Stream: An American Chronicle* (New York: Boni and Liveright, 1922), 237.

11. Caroline F. Ware, ed., *The Cultural Approach to History* (New York: Columbia University Press, 1940), 87.

12. Catharine R. Stimpson, "On Differences: Modern Language Association Presidential Address 1990," *Publications of the Modern Language Association,* May 1991, reprinted in Paul Berman, ed., *Debating P.C.: The Controversy over Political Correctness on College Campuses* (New York: Laurel, 1992), 44.

Chapter 9

1. William James, "On a Certain Blindness in Human Beings" and "What Makes a Life Significant," in *William James: Writings, 1878–1899* (New York: Library of America, 1992), 841–60, 861–80.

2. Griffith is quoted in Scott Simmon, *The Films of D. W. Griffith* (New York: Cambridge University Press, 1993), 52.

3. Thomas A. Bailey, "The Myths of American History," *Journal of American History* 55 (June 1968): 7–8; C. Vann Woodward, "A Short History of American History," *New York Times Book Review,* August 8, 1982.

4. Gertrude Himmelfarb, *The New History and the Old* (Cambridge: Harvard University Press, 1987), 17–18, 25–26, 56.

5. C. Vann Woodward, "The Fall of the American Adam," in Woodward, *The Future of the Past* (New York: Oxford University Press, 1989), 123, 125. This essay was originally published in the American Academy of

Arts and Sciences *Bulletin* 35 (November 1981): 24–34. An abbreviated version, which retains the statements quoted here, has recently been published as "The Fall of the American Adam: Myths of Innocence and Guilt," *Social Studies Review* 12 (Fall 1992): 9–11. For Woodward's views on what he calls the "outburst of minority assertiveness in the United States," see Woodward, "Equal But Separate," a review of Arthur Schlesinger's *The Disuniting of America,* in the *New Republic* (July 15 and 22, 1991): 41–43. For examples of the term "oppression studies," see Roger Kimball, *Tenured Radicals: How Politics Has Corrupted Our Higher Education* (New York: Harper and Row, 1990), 19–21, and John Taylor, "Are You Politically Correct?" *New York Magazine* (January 21, 1991): 35.

6. Eric Foner, ed., *The New American History* (Philadelphia: Temple University Press, 1990), ix–x.

7. Robert Louis Stevenson, *Across the Plains* (London: Chatto and Windus, 1892), 206–28.

8. Ralph Ellison, *Invisible Man* (New York: Modern Library edition, 1952), 331–32.

9. Gunnar Myrdal, *An American Dilemma* (New York: Harper and Row, 1962), 928–29; Abram Kardiner and Lionel Ovesey, *The Mark of Oppression: Explorations in the Personality of the American Negro* (1951; Cleveland: Meridian, 1962), 384.

10. Fisk University, *Unwritten History of Slavery: Autobiographical Accounts of Negro Ex-Slaves,* Ophelia Settle Egypt, J. Masuoka, and Charles S. Johnson, eds. Unpublished typescript (Nashville: Social Science Institute, Fisk University, 1945), 45–46.

11. For more on the blues and the entire question of African American culture and the larger society, see Lawrence W. Levine, *Black Culture and Black Consciousness: Afro-American Folk Thought from Slavery to Freedom* (New York: Oxford University Press, 1977).

12. *New York Times,* editorials, July 8, 1921; January 28, 1928. See also editorials in the issues of April 26, 1920; January 30, 1922; and February 6, 1923.

13. *New York Times,* January 28, 1928.

14. Michael Novak, *The Rise of the Unmeltable Ethnics: Politics and Culture in the Seventies* (New York: Macmillan, 1972), 111.

Chapter 10

1. Lynn Cheney, *Telling the Truth: A Report on the State of the Humanities in Higher Education* (Washington, D.C.: National Endowment for the Humanities, September 1992), 7.

2. George F. Kennan, *Around the Cragged Hill: A Personal and Political Philosophy* (New York: Norton, 1993), 152.

3. Quoted in Gerard A. Postiglione, *Ethnicity and American Social Theory: Toward Critical Pluralism* (Lanham: University Press of America, 1983), 173.

4. For a convenient collection of recent scholarly views see Virginia Yans-McLaughlin, ed., *Immigration Reconsidered: History, Sociology, and Politics* (New York: Oxford University Press, 1990). An earlier but still very useful bibliographical essay is Rudolph J. Vecoli, "The Resurgence of American Immigration History," *American Studies International* 17 (Winter 1979): 46–66. For recent scholarship on women of various ethnicities, see Ellen Carol DuBois and Vicki L. Ruiz, eds., *Unequal Sisters: A Multicultural Reader in U.S. Women's History* (New York: Routledge, 1990). For two recent syntheses, see John Bodnar, *The Transplanted: A History of Immigrants in Urban America* (Bloomington: Indiana University Press, 1985) and Ronald Takaki, *A Different Mirror: A History of Multicultural America* (Boston: Little Brown, 1993). The Bodnar quote is on p. 216 of his book.

5. John Higham, "From Process to Structure: Formulations of American Immigration History," in Peter Kivisto and Dag Blanck, eds., *American Immigrants and Their Generations* (Urbana: University of Illinois Press, 1990), 11–41; David A. Hollinger, *Postethnic America: Beyond Multiculturalism* (New York: Basic Books, 1995); Gary B. Nash, "The Great Multicultural Debate," *Contention* 1 (Spring 1992): 1–28; Werner Sollors, *Beyond Ethnicity* (New York: Oxford University Press, 1986); Henry Louis Gates, Jr., "Pluralism and Its Discontents," *Contention* 2 (Fall 1992): 69–77; Michael Omi and Howard Winant, *Racial Formation in the United States from the 1960s to the 1980s* (New York: Routledge and Kegan Paul, 1986), 48, 138, 52.

6. Boorstin's views are in Tad Szulc, "The Greatest Danger We Face," *Parade Magazine*, July 25, 1993, 4–5; Arthur Schlesinger, Jr., *The Disuniting of America* (New York: Norton, 1992), 118, 112–13.

7. Papp is quoted in the *New York Times,* December 13, 1981, 1, 30; Glenn Ligon's etching is reproduced in Zoë Ingalls, "Cutting-Edge Art: Stretching Minds, Spurring Debates," *Chronicle of Higher Education,* January 12, 1996, B4–5; David M. Potter, *The South and the Sectional Conflict* (Baton Rouge: Louisiana State University Press, 1968), 48.

8. Schlesinger, *The Disuniting of America,* 82. For examples of the new historiography on slavery and African American culture in the United States, see John W. Blassingame, *The Slave Community: Plantation Life in the Antebellum South* (1972; rev. ed., New York: Oxford University Press, 1979); Ira Berlin, "Time, Space, and the Evolution of Afro-American Society on British Mainland North America," *American Historical Review* 85 (February 1980); Eugene Genovese, *Roll, Jordan, Roll: The World the Slaves Made* (New York: Pantheon, 1974); Lawrence W. Levine, *Black Culture and Black Consciousness: Afro-American Folk Thought from Slavery to Freedom* (New York: Oxford University Press, 1977); Albert Raboteau, *Slave Religion: The "Invisible Institution" in the Antebellum South* (New York: Oxford University Press, 1978); Peter H. Wood, *Black Majority: Negroes in Colonial South Carolina from 1670 through the Stono Rebellion* (New York: Knopf, 1974); Sterling Stuckey, *Slave Culture: Nationalist Theory and the Foundations of Black America* (New York: Oxford University Press, 1987); Gary Nash, *Red, White, and Black* (Englewood Cliffs: Prentice-Hall, 1974); Charles Joyner, *Down by the Riverside: A South Carolina Slave Community* (Urbana: University of Illinois Press, 1984); Mechal Sobel, *Trabelin' On: The Slave Journey to an Afro-Baptist Faith* (Westport: Greenwood Press, 1979) and *The World They Made Together: Black and White Values in Eighteenth-Century Virginia* (Princeton: Princeton University Press, 1987); Margaret Washington Creel, *A Peculiar People: Slave Religion and Community-Culture among the Gullahs* (New York: New York University Press, 1988); Shane White, *Somewhat More Independent: The End of Slavery in New York City* (Athens: University of Georgia Press, 1991); Herbert G. Gutman, *The Black Family in Slavery and Freedom, 1750–1925* (New York: Pantheon, 1976); Nathan Irvin Huggins, *Black Odyssey: The African-American Ordeal in Slavery* (New York: Oxford University Press, 1990); Leon F. Litwack, *Been in the Storm So Long: The Aftermath of Slavery* (New York: Alfred A. Knopf, 1979). For two book-length overviews of this historiography, see August Meier and Elliott Rudwick, *Black History and the His-*

torical Profession, 1915–1980 (Urbana: University of Illinois Press, 1986), and Peter J. Parish, *Slavery: History and Historians* (New York: Harper and Row, 1989).

9. Schlesinger, *The Disuniting of America,* 128–29; Lewis F. Feuer, "From Pluralism to Multiculturalism," *Society* 29 (November/December 1991): 21; Hugh Trevor-Roper, *The Rise of Christian Europe* (London: Thames and Hudson, 1965), 9–11.

10. Schlesinger, *The Disuniting of America,* 138.

11. Nathan Irvin Huggins, "The Deforming Mirror of Truth," published as the Introduction to the 1990 edition of *Black Odyssey,* xi–lxx. An abbreviated version appeared in *Radical History Review* 49 (Winter 1991): 25–46. See also, Lawrence W. Levine, "The Historical Odyssey of Nathan Irvin Huggins," *Radical History Review* 55 (Winter 1993): 113–32.

12. *Addresses at the Inauguration of Charles William Eliot as President of Harvard College, Tuesday, October 19, 1869* (Cambridge: Sever and Francis, 1869), 62.

13. Samuel Flagg Bemis, "American Foreign Policy and the Blessings of Liberty," *American Historical Review* 67 (January 1962): 291–305.

14. Alfred North Whitehead, *Symbolism: Its Meaning and Effect* (1927; New York: Fordham University Press, 1985), 87–88.

Epilogue

1. Karl Marx, *The Eighteenth Brumaire of Louis Bonaparte* (1852, 1869; New York: International Publishers, 1981), 15.

2. Richard J. Herrnstein and Charles Murray, *The Bell Curve: Intelligence and Class Structure in American Life* (New York: Free Press, 1994), 523–26.

3. Paul Ricoeur, "Civilizations and National Cultures," in Paul Ricoeur, *History and Truth,* quoted in Anthony Giddens, *The Consequences of Modernity* (Stanford: Stanford University Press, 1990), xi.

4. Ishmael Reed, "America: The Multinational Society," in *Multi-Cultural Literacy,* Rick Simonson and Scott Walker, eds. (Saint Paul: Graywolf Press, 1988), 160.

5. Jürgen Habermas, "The New Obscurity: The Crisis of the Welfare State and the Exhaustion of Utopian Energies," in Habermas, *The New Conservatism: Cultural Criticism and the Historians' Debate,* Sherry Weber Nicholsen, trans. (Cambridge: MIT Press, 1989).

Index

Library of Congress Cataloging-in-Publication Data

Levine, Lawrence W.
    The opening of the American mind : canons, culture, and history /
Lawrence W. Levine
        p.   cm.
    Includes bibliographical references and index.
    ISBN 0-8070-3118-6 (cloth)
        1. United States—Intellectual life.   2. Education, Higher—United
States.   I. Title.
E169.1.L5372 1996
001.1'0973—dc20   96-33866